High-Powered Teams

A Guide to
Getting the Most Out of Your
Student Team

Merida L. Johns, PhD

Published by Lulu Press

ISBN 978-1-4303-1364-9

http://www.MLJohnsPhD.com

Dedication

To my students, who have inspired me.

A Special Word of Thanks

Every book is a team effort, and this book is no exception.

Special thanks to Russell Johns for his encouragement and belief.

Thank you to my colleagues whose critique made this a better guide.
Dr. Marion Ball, Johns Hopkins University
Barbara Glondys, DeVry University
Dr. Gezinus Hidding, Loyola University Chicago
Pamela Oachs, The College of St. Scholastica
Dr. Nannette Sayles, Macon State College

Particular thanks to Pam Sourelis for her developmental and copyediting
work that helped made this guide possible.

Table of Contents

Introduction

Effective teams don't just happen!

 As a college student, I participated in many teams. For good reason, I always cringed when the instructor announced that a major portion of the final grade would be based on a group project.

The team experience was seldom a pleasant one, nor was it one that I believed increased my learning. In my student teams, no one knew who was in charge or what the ground rules were. Furthermore, we didn't know each other very well or know how to harness our skills and capabilities to get the job done.

Our team meetings were always awkward. We wasted hours in meetings that usually went in circles. No one on our team knew the skills for making a meeting productive. Some students tended to dominate the group; it was their way or the highway. Others didn't speak up or were afraid to share their ideas. Some members were happy to let others do the work for them. And then there was always at least one member who didn't show up for meetings, didn't turn in work on time, and simply was undependable.

1

In sports, successful teams have a game plan. But in my classroom teams, the game plan was missing. Unlike a sports team, our project teams did not identify team objectives or make a list of the tasks to be done or identify who was responsible for completing them. Without a task list, we couldn't lay out a logical sequence or timeline for completing our work. Consequently, we made up the game plan on the fly. This resulted in misunderstandings, poor communication, missed due dates, and arguments among team members.

Finally, of course, there was the question of equality. Who deserved getting the "A" grade on the project? Few of us wanted to acknowledge this 10,000-pound gorilla in the room, but we always held animosity for the slackers who never did their fair share of the work but got the good grade anyway.

After making the transition from college student to college professor, I was determined not to subject my students to the frustration I had experienced with working in student teams. But I knew that teams were an essential part of contemporary life and that students should learn how to effectively function in multi-disciplinary teams.

I was familiar with research showing that students learn more, remember it longer, and develop superior reasoning and critical thinking skills when they work in a cooperative learning and team environment. Why didn't I feel that my team members and I were learning more and developing better critical thinking skills by participating in a team project? The answer is that these teams were not well managed. We had set no ground rules for team operation. We didn't assess individual team member skills, and most importantly we didn't develop a game plan. For teams to work productively students must manage and take ownership of their teams.

So how do students manage their teams to achieve the best possible learning environment? Learning more about student cooperative learning (teams) from colleagues, by reading the literature on collaborative education, and by using a great deal of input from my own students, I developed a process to help students manage teams.

The process consists of several steps. These steps help students organize their teams, conduct productive meetings, optimize team member skills, and set ground rules for team operation. The steps also help students to identify, organize, and prioritize tasks, and to develop a timeline for completing them.

At the end of each semester, my students and I debriefed how the team process had gone. We identified what worked and what didn't work. For those areas that needed improvement, we identified remedies that would allow the teamwork to go more smoothly. Each semester I updated my course handouts to include these suggestions. Eventually I developed a comprehensive manual to help students get the most out of their student teams. As students took ownership of their teams and learned to manage them, course evaluations became more and more positive. In fact, students reported that they learned more by working in teams and liked it better than doing the work individually. Finally, the outcomes of a cooperative learning and team environment were being consistently achieved!

When other faculty members heard about how the students in my courses managed their own teams, they wanted to implement the same processes. However, a succinct guide with an explanation of the key processes that make up a well-managed, high-powered student team was not available. At the urging of faculty and students alike, I compiled my methods into the current manual, *High-Powered Teams: A Guide to Getting the Most Out of Your Student Team.*

This manual is for you to use in managing your college classroom teams effectively. The concepts and principles of managing teams transcend disciplines. This means that students in disciplines such as business, computer science, health services administration, engineering, and education, among others, will find the processes discussed in this manual helpful in managing a student team.

All of the strategies and steps in this manual apply to any type of team. It doesn't matter if the team is a virtual one where you work online or is campus-based and meets face-to-face. You will find that managing teamwork is a challenge no matter what type of team you are working in. Teamwork involves good planning, coordination, and the knowledge, input, and cooperation of many people. To achieve optimal work performance, you and your team, whether it is online or campus-based, must know where the project is going, how it will get there, and how to harness the skill set of all of your team members to work effectively.

Designing and implementing effective work teams is not rocket science, but it does require that you develop the skills and learn the strategies that are key for success. This guide is designed to help you to master these skills and essential strategies for creating productive, high-powered teams.

Chapter 1
Why Teams?

"The leaders who work most effectively…..never say 'I'.
They don't think 'I'. They think 'we';
They think team." (Tom Peters)

 Why should completing a class assignment as a team be a requirement in a college course? One reason is that for centuries people have seen that cohesive work groups performing interdependent tasks with common goals out-produce and outperform any random collection of individuals. We see examples of this in our everyday experience in community associations, athletic groups, and social institutions.

Another reason is that in today's world, businesses and organizations have found that establishing interdisciplinary teams is the most productive approach for making large-scale improvements.   Companies have learned that knowledge, experience, and information from a broad base of people are critical for decision-making and execution of project work.

Independent research supports this line of thinking. Results from studies show that successful teamwork increases employee communication and involvement in decision-making. This results in a company that is more flexible and can make changes more quickly and easily (Mohrman, Cohen,

& Mohrman, 1995). Studies also suggest that organizations are able to learn more effectively and retain this knowledge better when teams are used. In addition, employees who work in teams seem to feel better about decisions that they make themselves as opposed to those that are forced upon them. They are also more likely to implement decisions made collaboratively (West, Borrill, & Unsworth, 1998 as cited in Yancey, M., 2005). Businesses that use teams report improved productivity, safety, and employee attitude, and decreased absenteeism (Beverlein & Harris, 1998).

Because teamwork is key for almost every job in today's business world, it is important for students to learn how to work productively in teams. Some companies are using specific questions to assess a job candidate's skill in working in teams. The following questions, for example, appear in a human resources newsletter (Healthfield, 2006).

- Give an example of a successful project you were part of. What was your role? Why was the project successful?

- Describe two situations from your past work experience in which you have determined a team was the best potential solution to a problem, a needed process improvement, or a planned change. How did each work out?

- What actions and support, in your experience, make a team function successfully?

- Give me an example of a time when your work group or department worked especially well with another work group or department to accomplish a goal.

- Have you been a member of a team that struggled or failed to accomplish its goal? If so, what assessment did you make of the reasons for failure?

These questions aim to identify how well the job candidate will work as a member of a cross-functional or department team. They also assess the degree to which the candidate values teamwork and understands the reasons for team failure and success (Healthfield, 2006).

Some may argue that workplace teams are counter to the industrial way of life that promotes controlling and rewarding the individual. But the team philosophy has taken hold and is an acceptable structure for a majority of organizations today. With 51 percent of all employees on one kind of team or another, there is a business imperative for training people how to work in teams (Ozols, 1996).

In addition to the benefits derived from the use of teams in the business world, research has consistently demonstrated that students learn more, remember it longer, and develop superior communication, reasoning, and critical thinking skills through cooperative, team learning experiences (Gokhale, 1995). This is why the use of student teams should be incorporated into college courses.

8

Although technical competence is important, research shows that 85 percent of the reasons for teams succeeding or struggling have more to do with interpersonal issues and people skills (Cullen, 2006). These skills, such as communication, negotiation, and organization, can be learned. The purpose of this manual is to help you gain these skills. *What's in it for you?* Simply put, knowing how to create, work in, and manage a high-performance team will make you more competitive and valuable in the workplace.

References

Beyerlein, M. & Harris C. (1998). Introduction to Work-Teams, presentation at the 9th Annual International Conference on Work Teams.

Cullen, Susan. (August 2006). Checklist for High-Performing Teams. Retrieved February 24, 2007, from http://www.businessseek.biz/article-directory/article-524.html.

Gokhale, Anuradha A. (1995). Collaborative Learning Enhances Critical Thinking. *Journal of Technology Education*, 7, 1, 22-30.

Healthfield, Susan M. (2006). Teams and Team Work Job Interview Questions. Retrieved February 24, 2007 from http://humanresources.about.com/od/involvementteams/a/team_questions.htm.

Mohrman, S. A., Cohen, S. G. & Mohrman, Jr., A. M. (1995). *Designing team-based organizations: New forms for knowledge work*. San Francisco, CA: Jossey-Bass.

Ozols, V. (1996) Why Teams Don't Work. Rocky Mountain Quality Conference, Denver, Colorado, USA. Retrieved February 24, 2007 from http://www.ozols.com/teamsdontwork.htm.

Yancy, M. Work Teams Three Models of Effectiveness.
Retrieved February 24, 2007, from
http://www.workteams.unt.edu/literature/papermyancey.
html.

Chapter 2
Key Actions of High-Powered Teams

"A successful team beats with one heart." (Unknown)

 From experience as a student and as a college professor, I know that successful student teams don't just happen. Although strategies used to produce high-powered student teams may be simple, achieving success is not necessarily easy.

This chapter gives you an overview of nine key actions that will help make student teams successful. Then in the following chapters, each action is described in detail, with specific steps for implementing the action. If you use this set of key actions, your team is likely to be productive and high-powered.

Action 1: Solidify the Team Belief

A high-powered team believes that the simultaneous actions of separate team members together have greater total effect than the sum of their individual parts.

Many experts say that work in teams is counter to the American industrial society. Cooperation is the basis for the

11

success of any team, but the industrial era work culture traditionally promotes rewarding individual effort. In this culture, the usual work contract is the exchange of individual labor for individual pay.

Theories such as Taylor's Scientific Management, Skinner's Behavioral Model, and Maslow's Hierarchy of Basic Human Needs view the manager-worker association as a parent-child relationship (Koulikov, 1995). Even though today's workforce is more educated and innovative and may want to have more decision-making independence, there still remains the perception that, "I have my job and I am paid for my own efforts." I've seen this attitude prevail in most student teams as well. A common feeling in student teams is, "I don't want anyone else to profit from the work I put into a project." Or, "I don't want someone else getting a good grade because of my work." Before a student team can function effectively, this attitude must be overcome.

To work effectively, team members must embrace a belief in the value of the team. Solidifying team belief means that each team member accepts the following premises:

- A team is a group of individuals but is also a social entity.
- A team works toward a common goal, and the tasks that members perform are interdependent.
- Each member of the team acknowledges and respects the contribution of every other team member.

- Each member of the team contributes information, perspective, experience, and competencies to achieving the common goal.

In Chapter 3, your team will have the opportunity to do the "Lost on the Moon" exercise to solidify team belief.

Action 2:   Fit Team Talents and Size to the Tasks
A high-powered team matches team member talents and the size of the team to the tasks to be accomplished.

I have found that many student teams fail because the group composition is inappropriate. For example, the team might be too large or too small, or the team doesn't have the right mix of skills to get the project done. Student teams must be the right size, contain the right talents to accomplish the tasks, and have members diverse enough to learn from one another (Hackman, 1986).

Team size. When teams are too large, communication becomes complex. In large teams it is harder to create a culture of trust among members. This may result in cliques developing within the team. When teams are smaller, tasks are more likely to be completed. Although the number of team members depends upon the work to be performed, a team of five to six is ideal.

Right talents. A highly competent student who is matched with the wrong task can throw a team into a tailspin. Likewise, students who do not have the required competence can throw off team functioning. The student team must contain the correct skill set to perform team tasks. Chapter 3 discusses how you can identify and maximize the skill set in your student team.

Heterogeneity. Having a diverse team composed of a mixture of skills and skill levels provides opportunities for team members to learn from each other.

Chapter 3 describes in detail how you can organize your team and ensure that you respect and maximize team member skills.

Action 3: Define Team Mission & Establish Goals

A high-powered team defines its mission and identifies its goals to achieve purposeful work, coordination of effort, and efficient use of resources.

Henry Kissinger once said, "If you do not know where you are going, every road will get you nowhere." It's common sense that it's hard to get somewhere if you don't know where you are going! Yet student teams often fail because they have no clear mission or have not identified their goals.

Effective student teams require a clearly stated mission. A mission statement defines the team's purpose, identifies whom the team serves, and specifies the team's values about service, quality, and teamwork. The following is the mission statement of a student team in one of my classes:

14

Our mission is to use team management strategies to ensure a high-performing team that maximizes team members' skills in order to complete the course project that adheres to high quality standards and is delivered on time.

Clear, achievable goals are the companion pieces to the mission statement. Goals make teamwork purposeful, enhance coordination, and provide a basis for follow-up and reward. You can think of goals as statements that specify a level of performance, a deadline, or an objective. For example, for an information systems class project that requires the team to develop an inventory database, the following are possible goals:

- Within four-weeks deliver a relational database that catalogs inventory items.
- Within six-weeks, develop an end-user interface that allows inventory items to be added, deleted, or modified in the database.
- Within eight-weeks develop a user manual that trains users to enter, delete, or modify inventory items in the database.

Generally you will find that there are three benefits to setting goals for your team (Seijts and Latham, 2006). The first advantage is that goals keep your team focused on what is relevant. Goals like those above help prevent the team from going off on tangents, doing unnecessary work, and wasting time.

15

Goals also help your team allocate the appropriate amount of effort to the project. In the example above, the team knows that members must be allocated to three different tasks and that each of these has a specific deadline.

The third advantage of goals is that they keep your team motivated by laying out a roadmap of what needs to get done. Knowing what your team's goals are and meeting these goals helps to keep team morale high.

Chapter 4 provides additional examples, exercises, and information on developing a team mission and goals.

Action 4. Value Personal Style and Diversity
A high-powered team is composed of and values members with different work and personal styles.

It is a well-known fact that teams composed of a variety of people with different experiences and areas of expertise are usually more successful than those that do not have member diversity (Yancy, 2005). If teams don't have the right diversity and the team is lopsided, certain tasks will not be completed or even begun (Benjamin, 2005).

I have found, however, that diversity itself is not enough for a student team to succeed. Student teams that have been successful in my courses valued and respected the strength that diversity brought to their team.

When team members do not understand that people receive information, form opinions, and communicate with others in different ways, conflict can easily surface and lead to poor performance. For example, some people are excellent information gatherers but poor innovators. Others may be great at coming up with new ideas but are not good implementers. When student teams understand the various work and decision-making styles of their team members, the teams will be able to create their best work.

How can members value and respect the diversity in their teams? A number of assessment tools can be used to determine individual work and personality styles. Chapter 3 includes samples of some of these tools. You and your team members can use the results of these tools to form a more smoothly performing team (Mutchler, 1998).

Action 5: Establish Team Norms

A high-powered team establishes team norms and a means for holding each team member accountable to them.

As team members, we all have been frustrated with the person who arrives late to meetings or skips them altogether, doesn't turn work in on time, or completes work at the last possible minute. This type of behavior leads to poor team morale and poor work performance, and results in interpersonal conflict. To counteract these types of behaviors, student teams can establish requirements for behavior, called team norms.

17

Team norms are patterns of behavior and activities that form the ground rules for how team members will interact. A norm is a system of shared values, beliefs, and control systems to produce patterns of behavior. Norms have several benefits for student teams (Buchholz and Roth,1987):

- They communicate what behavior is expected.
- They help maintain order.
- They eliminate having to rethink every action.
- They provide a sense of security.

It is hard to hold individuals accountable for their behavior without written norms that have been agreed upon by team members. You should develop norms when your team begins to work together. If expected behaviors are not identified at the beginning, it is harder to bring everyone back into a cohesive working group when behaviors become disruptive.

Team norms can be divided into the following categories:

- **Meeting norms** address when, where, and how often to meet, and expectations of attendance, timeliness and preparation.
- **Relationship norms** set expectations for how team members treat each other.
- **Communication norms** explain how information is exchanged outside of meetings and during meetings, and what listening, information sharing, and communication behaviors are expected.

- **Leadership norms** set down the accountability of each team member for ensuring balanced participation and input from all members, and guide the team in making consensus decisions, resolving conflict, and keeping the team focused and on-task.
- **Task-related norms** outline expectations for quality of work, timeliness, and workload distribution standards.

When students create written expectations for behavior at the beginning, the team functions more productively, with less interpersonal conflict. Chapter 4 discusses how to develop team norms and include them in a team charter.

Action 6: Conduct Productive Meetings

High-powered teams identify meeting purpose and desired outcomes and use process controls to conduct meetings.

Approximately 25 million meetings are held daily in corporate America. About half of the meeting time is wasted (Moncrif, 2005)! From my experience working with students, this statistic is equally true for student team meetings. While meetings are an important part of a high-powered team, meeting mismanagement can result in wasted time, frustration, deflated energy, conflict, and lowered team morale.

Poor meetings share several characteristics. Among these are poor preparation, inadequate agendas, insufficient facilitation, ineffective decision making, rambling discussions, and domination by a few members. The good news is that poor meetings can be attributed primarily to poor process, and poor process can be corrected.

Chapter 5 covers the essentials of planning and conducting a productive meeting. In this chapter you will learn how to develop agendas, manage meetings, and compile meeting documentation.

Action 7. Promote Communication & Cooperation
High-powered teams use communication-encouraging behaviors to promote open communication and cooperation.

If you want your team to work well together, you must use open, constructive communication techniques. Ineffective student teams let communication problems produce stress and tension among team members, which lowers productivity (Montebello, 1994).

For example, when there is poor communication there are information gaps. Minus information, people make assumptions and try to figure out things based on their own experience and knowledge. They create explanations about why someone acted in a certain way or why someone did or did not do something. Misunderstandings occur when unsupported assumptions are acted upon as if they were true.

The most threatening assumptions to teamwork are about other's motives—why a team member did or did not do something.

In order for your team to function at a high level, it needs to have open communication, with no hidden agendas, and it needs to share information. You can build team communication and collaboration by refraining from using communication-stopping behaviors such as judging, manipulating, and controlling.

You can build communication by using communication-encouraging behaviors such as these:
- Speaking candidly
- Listening
- Acknowledging other's views
- Discussing similarities and differences in views
- Explaining perceptions
- Negotiating agreement

In Chapter 5 you will learn more about these communication-encouraging behaviors.

Action 8: Manage Conflict

High-powered teams manage conflict through mutual respect, willingness to resolve disputes, and effective communication.

Conflict frequently arises in student teams. In my experience as a college professor, I can't remember a time where conflict wasn't present in at least a few of the student teams in my classes. It may be surprising, however, to learn that several benefits can result from conflict. Conflict is a driving force of change. In fact, research shows that the work of a team depends on conflict in order to thrive and prosper (Coser,1956). The key is to effectively manage conflict. When teams manage conflict, many positive results occur. New ideas and creative problem solving can result from managed conflict.

But conflict in your student team can have a disruptive effect if it is not managed correctly (McDaniel, Littlejohn, & Domenici, 1998; Sessa, 1996). Team energy and relationships, and task accomplishment can be severely damaged as a result of unmanaged conflict. So how can you manage conflict in your student team?

Teams should not reduce conflict but learn how to handle it constructively (Rayeski and Bryant, 1994). To do this, team members must respect one another and be willing to resolve disputes. Principal ways of handling conflict that have worked in my student teams include using communication

techniques such as learning to confront others constructively, listening to other's concerns, acknowledging oppos-
ing perspectives, and responding appropriately.

Conflict management techniques that you can use are explored in more detail in Chapter 5.

Action 9: Manage the Project
High-powered teams use effective techniques to organ-
ize, define, plan, and manage the project.

Simply mastering the eight actions already discussed will
not make a winning team. To be effective you must inte-
grate the eight action items within a comprehensive plan
that manages the total team project. This means that you
need to put into practice the eight action items along with
techniques to identify what work needs to be done, when,
and by whom, as well as techniques to keep your project
on schedule.

The experience of hundreds of teams in my classes has
shown that student teams are successful when they use the
following steps to organize, define, plan, and manage their
team projects. As you read through the descriptions of
each of the steps, you will see how the action items already
discussed are incorporated. You will also learn about additional techniques to help plan your project work and keep it
on schedule.

Organizing the Team. The first step is to organize your team. Two of the actions we already talked about, solidifying the team belief and getting to know each other, are part of team organization. Team-building activities and various assessments are used to build team belief and identify the competencies and work and personal styles of each team member. Team organization consists of selecting the team leader, identifying team member responsibilities, and developing written team norms. The specifics on how to organize your team are covered in Chapter 3.

Developing the Team Charter. Once your team is organized, you need to set the ground rules for operation. A team charter is a written document developed by the team members that accomplishes this. The team charter serves as a contract among team members. Many elements compose a team charter. Some of these have already been described, such as developing the team mission, goals, and norms. Chapter 4 expands upon how you develop a team charter.

Conducting Productive Meetings. Team meetings are an essential part of making decisions and getting work done. However, a lot of wasted time and effort can result from poorly managed meetings. A high-powered team is one that makes sure it has good processes that ensure good outcomes. Using good processes in conducting meetings is essential. Chapter 5 provides details on how students in my classes were able to use simple techniques that resulted in highly productive meetings.

Defining the Project. I have found that one of the most common stumbling blocks that prevents student teams from succeeding is not clearly defining at the beginning of the project what work needs to get done. Defining a project provides a common understanding among all team members of the extent and nature of the project.

Chapter 6 provides examples and templates to help you define your team's project.

Planning the Project. Once your team is organized and has developed its charter and defined its project, it is time to put into place the details of how your project will be carried out.

Time and again, student teams fail because they have not taken time at the very beginning to identify what tasks need to be completed and the timeframe, resources, and communication mechanisms needed for the project. As the old saying goes, "The devil is in the details." To be successful, your team must attend to the details.

Chapter 7 gives examples and tools for you to use in planning your project work.

Managing Project Work. Managing project work involves tracking the team's progress in meeting its goals. Your team should hold interim meetings to assess task status and completion, scheduling, and resources needs. In your team meetings, you should identify problems and determine if task schedules and assignments need readjustment. You will prepare interim team reports that document the continuing status of the project and function as internal communication for the team. Project status reports are usually used as a means of communication to stakeholders outside of the project team and document progress to date compared with the original project plan.

Chapter 8 explains in more detail the tools you can use to manage your project.

Closing out and evaluating the project. Once your project is completed, your team must perform a number of closeout activities such as preparing a final project report and conducting a post project evaluation review.

In Chapter 9 more details are given to help you closeout and evaluate your project.

Summary

Successful student teams don't just happen. Achieving a high-powered team is not easy. However, all of strategies discussed above, if properly executed, make it easier for you to achieve a smooth-running and effective team.

The following chapters will guide you and your team through each of the strategies in a logical step-by-step process. Activities, templates, examples, and other tools are provided to help you achieve a smooth functioning and top performance team.

References

Benjamin, L. (2005) Why Teams Fail. Retrieved
February 24, 2007, from http://www.laurabenjamin.com/
articles/WhyeamsFail.htm

Buchholz, Steve and Roth, Thomas (1987). *Creating the
High-Performance Team.* New York: John Wiley and
Sons.

Coser, L. A. (1956). *The functions of social conflict.* Glen-
coe, IL: The Free Press.

Hackman, J. R. & Walton, R. E. (1986). Leading Groups in
Organizations. In Goodman, P. S. (Ed.). *Designing
Effective Work Groups,* 72-119. San Francisco, CA:
Jossey-Bass.

Koulikov, M. (2006). Facilitation of Teams in the Context of
Modern Industrial Development. Center for Collaborative
Organizations. University of North Texas. Retrieved
February 24, 2007 from http://www.workteams.unt.edu/
literature/paper-mkoulikov.html.

McDaniel, G., Littlejohn, S., & Domenici, K. (1998). A team
conflict mediation process that really works! In M. Bullock,
C. Friday, K. Belcher, B. Bisset, S. Hurley, C. Fotte, and
D. Thai (Eds.), *The International Conference on Work
Teams Proceedings: 1998* (pp. 67-74). Denton:
University of North Texas, Center for the Study of Work
Teams.

Moncrief, G. (2005). Meetings: Time Wasted or Well
Spent?. Retrieved February 24, 2007 from http://www.
enewsbuilder.net/theayersgroup/e_article000450602.cfm
?x+b11,0,w

Montebello, A.R. (1994). *Work Teams that Work Skills for
Managing Across the Organization.* Minneapolis: Best
Sellers Publishing.

Mutchler, Alyson. (2005). The Use of the Myers-Briggs Type Indicator and Team Management Systems in Teams. Center for the Study of Work Teams, University of North Texas. Retrieved February 24, 2007 from http://www.workteams.unt.edu/old/reports/Mutchler.html.

Rayeski, E., & Bryant, J. D. (1994). Team resolution process: A guideline for teams to manage conflict, performance, and discipline. In M. Beyerlein & M. Bullock (Eds.), *The International Conference on Work Teams Proceedings: Anniversary Collection. The Best of 1990 – 1994* (pp. 215-221). Denton: University of North Texas, Center for the Study of Work Teams.

Seijts, G.H., Latham, G.P.(2006). Learning goals or performance goals: Is it the journey or the destination? *The Ivey Business Journal.* 7(5). Retrieved February 24, 2007 from http://www.iveybusinessjournal.com/archives/

Sessa, V. I. (1996). Using perspective taking to manage conflict and affect in teams. *Journal of Applied Psychology,* 32(1), pp. 101-115.

Yancy, M. (2005) Work Teams: Three Models of Effectiveness (2005). Retrieved February 24, 2007 from http://www.workteams.unt.edu/literature/paper-myancey.html.

Chapter 3
Organizing the Team

*"A small group of committed people can make a difference
and change the world." (Margaret Mead)*

 You have just been assigned to
a student team to complete a
course project. Likely, your
instructor has given you
parameters for the team project.
These might include project background, expected deliverable, due date, and evaluation criteria.

How does your team go about tackling your assigned project? Before any other work is done, your team must organize it self. Challenges to team organization are discussed in this chapter. At the end of the chapter are two exercises to help your team organize itself.

Challenges to Team Organization

Several challenges present themselves in the organizing phase. These include previous poor experiences with teams, bias against teamwork, and uncertainty.

Team Experience. Before I make assignments to student teams, I ask my class, "How many of you have found that working in student teams has been one of your best academic experiences?" Invariably no one raises a hand!

Team experiences have been poor for many students. Students usually report that the problems they have faced on student teams include such things as:

- High degree of conflict
- Lack of communication
- Social loafing
- Dissatisfaction

These experiences create a preconceived notion that student teams can't work well. Later in the chapter, you and your team members will learn how you can change this perception.

Bias Against Teamwork. It is possible that some students have a bias against working in a team. Some students may object to working in teams because most of their education has been based on individual effort. They feel uncomfortable helping others or seeking help themselves. To overcome this bias, you will learn later in this chapter how to solidify "team belief" among all of your team members.

High Uncertainty. There is always uncertainty when a team is first created. Likely, your team is either a randomly assigned group of students or is formed out of "convenience" by selecting people sitting close to each other. It is unlikely that everyone knows each other's personality and work styles, work background, or personal interests. In addition, team members are asking themselves questions such as these:

- Will I fit in with this team?
- Who are these other people?
- Can we work well together?
- What will I be responsible for?

Steps in Organizing Your Team

To counter the biases and uncertainties, your team needs to do the following two things at its first team meeting:

- Solidify the belief that teamwork has value.
- Understand the personal styles of team members.

Step 1: Solidify Team Belief. Why should your team solidify team belief? For centuries, cohesive work groups with interdependent tasks and common goals have proven that they can out-produce and outperform any individual or any random collection of individuals. Basically the old adage that "two heads are better than one" holds true.

You and your team members must embrace the belief that the team has value. This is called *team belief.* Elements of team belief include:

- Seeing the team as a social entity
- Committing to achieving a common goal
- Acknowledging that each member of the team adds information, perspective, experiences, and competencies to achieve a common goal
- Accepting the interdependency of the tasks
- Respecting the contribution of every team member

31

Teambuilding exercises are used to build team belief by demonstrating how a wide level of support helps to achieve a common goal.

Your team should complete Exercise 3.1 to help develop team belief.

Exercise 3. 1. Lost on the Moon Team Building

Approximate Time to complete: 60 minutes

Directions: Each team member should read the Lost on the Moon scenario below and then answer the question that follows. Spend 15 minutes on this activity.

After completing the answers individually, work as a team and reach a consensus on the ranking of each of the items. Keep track of the teams' answers on the worksheet.

After the team has completed the activity, use the Lost on the Moon answer sheet in the Appendix to tally both the team's score and each individual's score.

Compare the team's score to each individual's score and then as a group answer the discussion questions on page 34. Spend 20 minutes on this activity.

Lost on the Moon Scenario

Your spaceship has just crashed on the moon. You were scheduled to rendezvous with a mother ship 200 miles away on the lighted surface of the moon, but the rough landing has ruined your ship and destroyed all the equipment on board except for the 15 items listed below.

Your crew's survival depends on reaching the mother ship, so you must choose the most critical items available for the 200-mile trip. Your task is to rank the 15 items below in terms of their importance for survival. Place a number 1 by the most important item, a number 2 by the second most important, and so on, through number 15, the least important.

32

Your Rank	Team Rank	Items
		Box of matches
		Food concentrate
		50 feet of nylon rope
		Parachute silk
		Solar-powered portable heating unit
		Two .45caliber pistols
		One case of dehydrated milk
		Two 100-pound tanks of oxygen
		Stellar map (of the moon's constellations)
		Self-inflating life raft
		Magnetic compass
		5 gallons of water
		Signal flares
		First-aid kit containing injection needles
		Solar-powered FM receiver-transmitter

Team Discussion

Check your answers with NASA's answer sheet in the Appendix. Compare your scores on the answer sheet to the team's score. In all of the classes where my students have completed this exercise, the team score was always better than any individual's score. This team-building exercise demonstrates that working in teams can have a better outcome than working individually.

As a group, discuss the following questions to help your team assess the value of working in a team.

- What do the differences between your individual answers versus the team's answers say about teamwork?
- How did team members reach consensus?
- How did the experience, perspective, and skills of team members help to achieve the common goal?
- Did team members depend upon each other in solving the problem?
- Has this exercise solidified the following beliefs about teams?
    o The team is a social entity.
    o Each member must commit to achieving the common goal.
    o Each member adds value to the team.
    o Each member's work is interdependent with every other team member's work.
    o The contribution of each member is important.

Step 2: Understand Personal Styles: The second step in organizing your team is to understand the personal styles of each team member. This will help strengthen your team, match style strengths to team tasks, and help reduce conflict.

Your team is composed of people with different experiences, areas of expertise, and personal styles. Some of your team members may be idea persons, others may be implementers, and still others may be detailed oriented. While diversity is what makes teams strong, conflict can surface and lead to poor performance when team members do not understand that differences exist in the way people receive information, form opinions, and communicate.

Everyone on a team must value and respect the strength that diversity brings to the team. Equally important, teams must recognize that if they lack certain traits, it will be difficult for them to complete, or in some cases to begin, tasks. Several types of tools are used to determine how people view their world and how they make decisions. Many of the popular assessments are based on the work of Carl Jung and the work of Isabel Briggs Myers and Katherine Briggs.

To assess your team members' personal styles, we are using an instrument based called TypeFocus. Before doing the assessment, you need to understand some basics about the assessment pairs the instrument uses. Assessment instruments that are based on Carl Jung's theories have four categories. Each category has two styles, and a descriptive tag is given to each style. These include:

- *What environment (world) do you prefer?* Do you prefer being out in the world and being with people (Extrovert) or are you more comfortable being alone and doing things on your own (Introvert)?

- *How do you prefer to handle information?* Do you prefer to have all the facts and look at details and then form a big picture (Sensor), or do you like to see the big picture first and then find out the facts (Intuitive)?
- *How do you like to make decisions?* Do you like to make decisions with your head, analyze the pros and cons and be logical in decision making (Thinker), or do you like to make decisions with your heart and are concerned most with maintaining harmony (Feeler)?
- *Do you like things structured or unstructured*? Are you task oriented, like to get things done and like to avoid rushing before a deadline (Judger), or do you like to be unstructured and casual and are stimulated by an approaching deadline (Perceiver)?

It is not hard to see that if you have team members who have opposite styles, conflict can easily arise. For example, a "Sensor" who likes to look at details before forming the big picture would likely conflict with an "Intuitive" who likes to form the big picture first before dealing with details.

It is also clear that if all team members have the same style, completing tasks might be difficult. For example, if everyone on your team is a "Perceiver" deadlines may not be met.

Determine your team's personal styles by completing Exercise 3.2.

Exercise 3.2. Understand Personal Style

The team can take the online computer assessment recommended below or another one provided by the instructor.

Once assessments have been completed, the team can reconvene and complete the exercises that follow.

Computer Assessment

TypeFocus offers a free assessment of personal style based on the preferences that are listed above. Each team member can take this personal assessment on his or her own.

Go to http://www.typefocus.com/index.html, the TypeFocus website. At the home page, click on "Free Assessment" and follow the instructions for taking the personal style assessment. The assessment contains about 60 items and will take you about 10 minutes to complete.

At the conclusion of the assessment, your personal style in each of eight categories will be determined. Print out a copy of your assessment to complete the following exercise:

Understanding Your Team's Personal Styles

Approximate Time to Complete: 30 minutes

1. Each member should share his or her personal style with the group.
2. Using the illustration on the following page, plot each member's style in each of the pie sections. Use the initial of the team member's first name to plot the style in each category. If the style score is low in a category, plot the individual's initial close to the center of the chart. If the score is high, plot the initial farther to the outside of the chart.

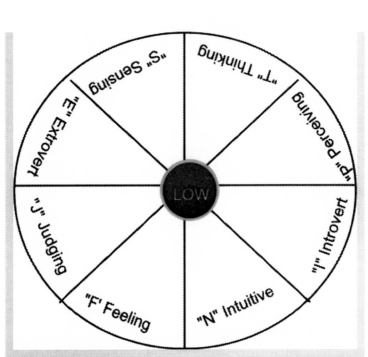

3. After plotting the team's personal styles, answer the following questions.

    - How diverse are the team members?
    - Does the team have enough diversity? If not, how will the team handle any gaps in style?
    - What are individual member's strengths?
    - How can the team maximize individual strengths to achieve a common goal?
    - Where might conflicts occur?
    - Based on personal style, who might be the best choice for team leader?

Using Style Diversity to Create a High-Powered Team

Using the team's style inventory does not stop with the initial assessment. On the contrary, information about personal styles will help your team do the following:

- Select a team leader
- Match style strengths to team tasks
- Respect the value of each team member
- Reduce team conflict

Select a Team Leader. Assuming the instructor allows teams to choose their own leaders, the team should use the personal style inventory to help make this decision.

The team leader should have several strengths to guide the team. Among these are trustworthiness and reliability. The leader should function in an orderly and purposeful manner and be an analytical thinker. The leader should be able to handle ambiguity and uncertainty and keep a cool head. A leader is committed to the team, is fair with team members, and keeps team goals in focus at all times. Coaching and communication skills are important as well as an ability to deal with people's feelings.

The team, however, should not exclusively use the style inventory to make the team leader selection. The team should also take into account qualities such as a good track record in leading other teams and a willingness to serve.

Match Style Strengths to Team Tasks. After the team has identified the project tasks that must be performed, they can use the style inventory to match tasks with the strengths of team members. For example, an interviewing task would be better assigned to an Extrovert than an Introvert. A task that deals with numerical details might better be assigned to a Sensor than an Intuitive. Chapter 7 discusses how to match personal style with tasks.

Reduce Team Conflict. A good way to remember each team member's dominant strength during team meetings is to display name cards that also include each person's dominant style. Knowing your team members' styles can reduce conflict. Consider the following scenario:

Your team is solving a problem. One of your team members, whose strength is an "I" (Intuitive), keeps leaping between different ideas and possibilities. Another team member, who is an "S" (Sensor), wants to work with facts, not ideas, to solve the problem. The Sensor member is becoming extremely frustrated with the Intuitive's problem-solving approach. Rather than get in an argument, the Sensor can say to the Intuitive, "Your "I" is showing too much. Let's bring the discussion around and look at some facts to approach the problem." Instead of attacking the individual, this approach acknowledges the characteristics of team members and lets them know that their personal style at the moment may be inhibiting progress. This strat-

egy has been used successfully in many student classes to reduce potential conflict.

Develop A Project Notebook

To organize, plan, and manage the class project, the team needs to compile a project notebook. The notebook can be in paper form, such as a three-ring binder, or in electronic form. The purpose of the notebook is to catalog and maintain all documentation related to the team and to the project.

Why is a project notebook important? First, it serves as the repository of the team's work. As the repository, it is the principal mechanism for sharing information among team members and other project stakeholders. The notebook serves as a reference guide during team meetings because it documents what happened, when it happened, and what decisions were made. Using the notebook as a reference guide minimizes misunderstandings and team conflict. The notebook provides documentation for the instructor and your team to assess and evaluate how well the project was organized, planned, and managed.

You might ask what is the difference between a project notebook and the final course project report? The project notebook documents how you carried out the project; the final project report documents what you accomplished.

Appendix B contains a description of the contents of a project notebook. Complete Exercise 3.3 below to begin developing your project notebook.

Exercise 3.3. Develop a Project Notebook

Refer to Appendix B to develop your project notebook. The notebook can be in paper or electronic form. Whatever its form, however, the notebook must be available for all team meetings and to all team members. If it is in electronic form, is should be posted to a project web board.

The team leader or secretary is usually responsible for maintaining the team master notebook. However, in many classes, each team member maintains a complete copy of the project notebook. This practice is valuable because each team member has a copy of the notebook after the course is finished and can use it as part of an individual portfolio and evidence of experience when seeking employment.

The following documentation from activities in this chapter should be placed in the project notebook:
- Lost on the Moon Exercise Results and Team Discussion
- List of team members and their personal styles

Technology Tools

There are a number of technology tools that you can use for organizing, managing, and handling communications. A description of these tools is provided in Appendix F.

Summary

Using activities that promote the valuing of team belief and team diversity is important for development of successful student teams.

High-powered teams understand that cooperation is the basis for success. To work effectively, all team members must embrace a belief in the value of the team. Teams composed of a variety of people with different experiences and areas of expertise are usually more successful than teams that do not have member diversity.

Steps that create cooperation among team members include:

- Solidifying team belief through team building exercises
- Identifying individual personal styles
- Determining the degree of team diversity
- Assessing how to use team diversity to achieve a high-powered team.

Chapter 4

Developing the Team Charter

Coming together is a beginning, staying together is progress, and working together is success. (Henry Ford)

 A team charter is a written agreement among your team members about the team's mission and goals, and the ground rules for operating as a team. The charter is a powerful document because it gives purpose and direction to your team and spells out boundaries and expected behaviors.

Since the charter sets the purpose and direction for your team, it needs to be the first activity the team completes after solidifying team belief and understanding personal styles. The charter is typically developed during the team's second meeting.

The charter needs to be specific to your team, reflecting the team's purpose and the team members' values. The charter's power comes from discussions of and agreement on the team's ground rules.

The following are the usual items contained in a team charter:

- Team name
- Team mission statement
- Team goals
- Team norms
- Team roles

Each of the above is discussed in the following pages. At the conclusion of the chapter, your team will complete an exercise that will help you develop your team charter.

Name Your Team

Naming and identity go hand-in-hand. The team name and logo should reflect the attributes the team feels are important. The following are examples of classroom team names:

- Collegiate Consultants
  - Represented the students' college environment as well as their idealism
- Quality Design and Consulting
  - Represented the team's focus on quality
- SMT Consulting
  - Represented the last initial of each team member's name.

Establish Your Team Mission

A clearly written mission statement defines the team's purpose, identifies who the team serves, and specifies the team's values about service, quality, and teamwork.

An effective mission statement provides vision and direction for your team. The mission statement is a brief statement that concisely describes the reason your team was formed and its purpose. The following are examples of clearly written mission statements developed by student teams:

- The mission of Collegiate Consultants is to successfully manage a team project and fulfill course requirements for developing a prototype computer application that meets the quality and functionality specifications of the class client.
- Quality Design and Consulting is a team formed to enhance each other's capabilities, develop each other's team management skills, and complete a class project in database development that adheres to high quality, reliability, and safety standards.

You can see that these mission statements provide a vision and direction for the team. They also describe the reason the team was formed and its purpose.

Identify Your Team Goals

Goals are the companion pieces to the mission statement. A goal specifies action and includes a specified level of performance and time frame for achievement. Goals must be attainable (don't set goals you can't possibly achieve) and relevant (all goals should be related to your team's mission).

Goals help keep your team focused. For example, look at the team goals below that were developed by one student team. Notice how the goals are specific and attainable and support the team's mission statement cited above.

The goals of Quality Design and Consulting are to

- Value the contribution of all team members in completing the course project
- Treat all members with respect
- Complete the database course project on time and at an "A" grade quality level.
- Achieve 100% attendance at all team meetings by all team members.
- Complete all project milestones on time 100% of the time.

Establish Your Team Norms

Team norms are patterns of behavior and activities that form the ground rules for how team members will interact and work together. Norms publicize a system of shared values, beliefs, and controls that moderate team behaviors.

Norms are an important strategy for minimizing situations where team members have not carried their fair share of the work. Norms are a way of managing team behavior. Norms also provide a benchmark for evaluating how well each team member worked on the team and how well she or he contributed to the final team project. Throughout the course, you will be able to evaluate how well each of your team members did in meeting each team norm.

You will want to develop norms for your team that include all of the following:

- Meeting norms
- Relationship norms
- Communication norms
- Leadership norms
- Decision-making norms
- Conflict-management norms
- Task-related norms

Meeting Norms. Meeting norms include behaviors, expectations, and activities associated with team meetings. The following are some examples of meeting norms developed by student teams:

- Team meetings will be held every Tuesday evening from 7:00-8:30 pm.
- The project leader will facilitate team meetings.
- Team members are expected to:
  o Attend all meetings
  o Be on time to meetings
- A meeting will have an agenda developed by the team leader. The meeting agenda will be distributed by email to all team members at least two days in advance of each team meeting.

- Minutes will be kept of all team and sub-team meetings and distributed to all team members within three days after the meeting.

Relationship Norms. Behaviors and expectations of how team members will act on the team and with each other are considered relationship norms. To ensure that all members are treated equitability and with respect, your team must develop relationship norms. The following are examples of relationship norms developed by student teams:

All team members will:
- Maintain a superior level of professionalism and not bring personal issues into a team meeting
- Contribute ideas and solutions
- Recognize and respect the differences in personal style in others
- Be flexible and respect the partnership created by the team and strive to achieve a "win-win" situation

Communication Norms. Communication norms are behaviors and activities related to how team members exchange ideas and information and maintain contact with each other. Contact information, including phone numbers, email, and addresses, for all team members should be gathered and placed in the team charter.

Frequent problems arising in student teams are the result of poor communication among team members. To reduce potential conflict, develop communication norms for your team. The following are examples of communication norms developed by student teams:

- The primary form of communication among team members is a dedicated Web bulletin board that is accessible to all team members at all times. Every team member is expected to log in to the bulletin board each weekday, read and make appropriate posts, and attach project files.
- The secondary means of communication includes email and telephone. The project leader will be copied on all project-specific emails. The initiator of a phone call must log a summary of the call on the Web bulletin board.

Leadership Norms. Leadership norms include team member and team leader responsibilities for promoting fairness, balance, and an environment conducive for collaboration. Teams that have leadership norms are less likely to engage in unhealthy conflict. The following are examples of leadership norms developed by student teams:

Every team member is expected to:

- Ensure that the team is striving for excellence in all facets of the project
- Guide the team in making consensus decisions, resolving conflict, and keeping the team focused on its task

- Create an environment that is conducive to open participation

Decision-Making Norms. These norms are expectations and ground rules for making team decisions. It is important that your team decide ahead of time how decisions are going to be made. Knowing the ground rules for decision making reduces misunderstandings and conflict. The following two examples illustrate decision-making norms from two different student teams.

- The project leader will seek consensus from team members on decisions affecting the outcome of the course project and/or management of the project. When agreement cannot be reached by consensus, the decision will be determined by majority vote of those present at the meeting.
- Decisions made at team meetings: All decisions affecting the outcome or management of the course project will be determined by majority vote of team members. All votes must take place during regularly scheduled team meetings with at least three of the five team members present.

Conflict-Management Norms. Ground rules for avoiding disagreements and arguments are called conflict-management norms. Teams that use conflict-management norms are more likely to engage in healthy debate rather than arguments. The following are examples of conflict-management norms:

- Do not interrupt another member.
- Acknowledge valid points made by team members.
- Accept all ideas as valid when presented.
- Build on each other's ideas.
- Do not dismiss any idea without exploring it.
- Do not make personal attacks on another member.
- Call a time-out if discussions are heated or going in circles.

Task-Related Norms. These norms include behaviors re-lated to team member responsibilities for task completion. You can assign specific task-related norms to the team leader and to team members. The following are examples of task-related norms:

- The team leader is responsible for:
  o Developing and distributing meeting agendas
  o Facilitating team meetings
  o Coordinating team tasks
  o Maintaining the project notebook
  o Submitting weekly written reports to the course instructor
- All team members are responsible for:
  o Completing tasks on time at a high-quality level
  o Coming prepared to all meetings
  o Participating in all meetings, sharing informa-tion, and providing input

o   Ensuring a balanced workload among team
    members

Assign Team Roles

Your team needs to assign specific tasks for organizing,
monitoring, and evaluating work to ensure a smoothly running team. You do this by developing an organizational
structure to delegate these responsibilities to people on
your team. The type of class project determines what key
roles are needed. For example, in a complex course project
where the team might consist of seven or more members,
there may be a team leader and several sub-project leaders. In smaller teams, there may be a team leader and a
team secretary. At the minimum, every team should have a
team leader and a team secretary.

Team Leader. The leader of a team should be a collaborative leader. This is different from leaders in a hierarchal
structure. The collaborative team leader guides rather than
controls and motivates rather than directs. Collaborative
leaders safeguard the process (the norms established by
the team) and facilitate interaction (Carter, 2006).

Team leaders are usually responsible for the following ac-
tivities:
- Preparing and distributing meeting agendas
- Facilitating team meetings
- Guiding activities of the team
- Making team assignments

- Coordinating team activities
- Tracking team progress

Team Historian. Documentation is an important part of team function. Documents such as agendas, meeting minutes, progress reports, timelines, and evaluations must be maintained in a team notebook. The historian can be responsible for collecting and keeping all of these materials together. The team notebook is usually submitted to the instructor at the end of the course.

Team Secretary. Meeting minutes must be taken for every team meeting. Some teams rotate the secretary task among all team members, with the exception of the team leader. This gives all members experience in the task and balances the workload. At the beginning of the project, the team makes the decision to rotate the function or give it to a specific team member for the entire course.

Develop Your Team Charter

Exercise 4.1 on the next page guides your team through the process of developing a team charter. Use the format in Figure 4.1 to write your team charter.

Exercise: 4.1.   Develop Your Team Charter

Approximate time: 2 hours

The agenda for the second team meeting should be to develop the team charter. If a team leader has not been already appointed, a team member should serve as interim team leader and facilitate the process of team charter development.   Team members should be prepared to make decisions on the following:

- ❖   Team Name

- ❖   Team Mission Statement

- ❖   Team Goals

- ❖   Team Norms

  - o   Meeting Norms

  - o   Relationship Norms

  - o   Communication Norms

  - o   Leadership Norms

  - o   Decision-Making Norms

  - o   Conflict-Management Norms

  - o   Task-Related Norms

- ❖   Team Roles

  - o   Team Leader

  - o   Team Historian

  - o   Team Secretary

Use the agenda below for developing your charter. Use the format in Figure 4.1 to develop the charter and include all of the elements listed. All team members must agree with the charter contents and sign the charter.

Once it is developed, every team member should receive a written copy of the team charter. Remember, the charter spells out the ground rules for team operation. The charter should be used as a reference throughout the course to ensure that all ground rules are being followed.

Sample Agenda for Team Charter Development

Time Allocation	Topic
10 minutes	Team Name
25 minutes	Team Mission
25 minutes	Team Goals
60 minutes	Team Norms & Roles

55

Figure 4.1. Team Charter Format

Team Charter

Our team charter is an agreement among our team members about our team mission and goals and the ground rules for behavior and operation.
Date Approved:

Course Name:

Team Members:

Team Name:
Reflects the attributes the team feels are important

Team Mission:
Defines the team's purpose and values about service, quality, and team-work

Team Goals:
Specific actions with performance level and time frames

Norms:
Behavior and ground rules for team interaction

Meeting Norms: Ground rules for team meetings

Relationship Norms: Expectation for how team members treat each other

Communication Norms: Ground rules for regular contact with each other for information and idea exchange

Leadership Norms: Behaviors for promoting fairness, team work balance, and cooperation

Decision-Making Norms: Ground rules for making team decisions

Conflict-Management Norms : Guidelines for handling and avoiding dys-functional arguments and conflict

Task-Related Norms: Responsibility regarding assignments

Team Roles: List responsibilities of team leader, secretary, historian, and other roles.

Signature of each team member

Exercise 4.2. Add to the Team Project Notebook

Your team should have developed a project notebook as part of Exercise 3.3 in Chapter 3.

Using Appendix B as a guide, add a copy of the team charter to the team project notebook.

Summary

A team charter is a written agreement among team members about the team mission and goals, and the ground rules for operating as a team. The charter is a powerful document because it gives purpose and direction to the team and spells out boundaries and expected behaviors.

Establishing the team charter is one of the first action items the team performs; the charter includes:

- Team name
- Team mission statement and team goals
- Team ground rules, including norms for meetings, relationships, communication, leadership, decision making, conflict management, and task management
- Team roles, including those for team leader, team historian, and secretary

References

Carter, Madeline. (2006). The Importance of Collaborative lLeadership in Achieving Effective Criminal Justice Outcomes. Center for Effective Public Policy. Department of Justice National Institute of Corrections. Retrieved from: http://www.collaborativejustice.org/docs/TheImportance%20of%20 Collaborative%20Leadership.doc.

Chapter 5
Conducting Productive Meetings and Handling Conflict

Any meeting worth holding is worth planning.

 Meetings are an important function of high-powered teams. Planning how to carry out a class project and decisions relating to the project are all handled through team meetings. Poorly managed meetings, however, can result in wasted time, frustration, deflated energy, team conflict, and inability to meet your team goals. Poor meetings are usually the result of poor process. To assure positive outcomes, your team should use the following three processes:

- Prepare for the meeting
- Manage the meeting
- Complete follow-up action

This chapter describes each of the above processes to help your team conduct productive meetings. Templates, checklists, and exercises are included throughout the chapter to guide your team in learning how to use good process to conduct productive meetings.

Prepare for the Meeting

Your team charter should identify the time, place, and frequency of regular team meetings. Additional meetings may also be required. Regardless of the type of meeting, preparing for any meeting involves the following:

- Determining meeting type
- Sending out meeting notification to members
- Developing and distributing a meeting agenda and resource materials
- Preparing materials and supplies

Determine Meeting Type. The purpose of team meetings is to share information and make decisions. Usually team meetings are held face-to-face. However, meetings can be conducted via conference call or online. Conference calls and online meetings are useful to exchange information, answer questions about reports, or update members on the team's progress in meeting milestones. Face-to-face meetings are useful when the team needs to share ideas and opinions, brainstorm, problem solve, and make decisions. The team should determine which method is best for conducting team business.

Send out Meeting Notification. The team leader is responsible for calling team meetings. Meeting participants must be notified in advance of the meeting, regardless of whether the meeting is a face-to-face meeting, a conference call, or an online meeting. For regular team meetings, the meeting date, time, and place for the next meeting should be identified at the conclusion of each meeting. Notification for ad hoc or special meetings must be made well in advance to give meeting participants time to make arrangements to attend. The team leader, or other designated person, is responsible for notification for ad hoc meetings. Meeting norms in the team charter should specify how far in advance regular and ad hoc meeting notification should be made.

Develop Meeting Agenda. Because the agenda is the road map for the meeting, every meeting must have a pre-published agenda. A well-prepared agenda provides participants with information about the beginning and ending times of the meeting, what topics will be discussed and voted upon, who is responsible for leading the topic discussions, and the time frame for each topic. Agenda items should be clear and specific. Figure 5.1 is an example of a meeting agenda.

Notice that the agenda specifies the date and place of the meeting and meeting start and end times. Each topic is clearly defined with a specific time period allocated to it and with an identified facilitator. Also note that each topic is written with a verb and indicates what action or decision is to take place.

Your team leader should prepare the agendas and distributes these in advance of the meeting. This allows proper notification to team members of the topics to be raised during the meeting and sets the expectation that everyone will come to the meeting prepared. The team charter should specify how far in advance agendas should be distributed.

Figure 5.1. Sample Agenda

Agenda Regular Meeting Collegiate Consultants December 14, 2006 Place: Collegiate Library, Study Room 487		
Time	Topic	Facilitator
7:00 PM	Meeting Convenes Approval of Minutes of 12/1/06	Paul
7:05	Determine Project Scope	Paul
7:30	Finalize draft diagram of current system	Judy
7:50	Finalize function review of new system	Lucia
8:15	Determine functions that fit within project scope	Chuck
8:30	Make assignments for: Flow diagram, entity relation- ship, and use case develop- ment	Heather
8:45 9:00 PM	Action Items for next meeting Meeting adjourns	Paul

Resources. Resources needed for information or decision making should be distributed prior to the meeting. For example, in the agenda in Figure 5.1, the minutes of the previous meeting and the draft diagram of the current system should be distributed prior to the meeting. This allows team members time to review information and come prepared to make decisions. Preparing and distributing materials prior to the meeting will shorten meeting times because team members will have time to analyze information in advance. The meeting norms in the team charter should specify how far in advance of the meeting resource materials and the meeting agenda are distributed.

Materials and Supplies. Your team should identify what materials and supplies are needed for each meeting. For example, arrangements should be made for materials such as flip charts, laptop computers, and overhead projectors.

Manage the Meeting

In addition to good preparation, a productive meeting must also be conducted well. Both the team leader and team members are responsible for ensuring that the meeting is well managed.

Role of the Team Leader. The goal of each meeting is to accomplish the agenda objectives, make decisions, and determine action items linked to positive results.

As the meeting chair, the team leader must have a positive attitude, empower participants, and be impartial in treating both issues and meeting participants. As meeting chair, the team leader assumes the following responsibilities:

- **Takes charge of the proceedings**. The team leader guides the group through the meeting agenda and makes sure that each agenda item is fully addressed. The team leader makes certain that team meeting norms are observed during the meeting process.

- **Develops and distributes the agenda.** The team leader develops the agenda and distributes it to all participants before the meeting. The time frame in which the agenda is distributed is determined by the team's meeting norms.

- **Starts and ends the meeting on time.** The team leader makes sure that the meeting starts and ends on time. If it appears that business will not be accomplished in the allotted time, the chair can ask members for permission to extend the meeting in increments of five minutes or carry over business to the next meeting.

- **Follows established meeting rules.** Meeting norms should be listed in the team's charter. The team leader is responsible for making sure that all meetings follow these norms. The following are examples of meeting norms:
  - Meetings start and end on time.
  - No one member dominates the meeting.
  - Everyone participates in the meeting.
  - Everyone comes prepared to the meeting.
  - Agendas are distributed by email two days in advance of the meeting.
  - All decisions are made by a majority vote.

- A majority of members must be present to conduct business at a meeting.

These are only a few examples of meeting norms. Your team should develop its own norms.

- **Follows the agenda and time frame.** In taking charge of the proceedings, the team leader makes sure the agenda is followed, including adhering to time frames for each topic. The team leader usually appoints another team member to serve as "time-keeper." The timekeeper's task is to monitor the time spent on each topic, alert the team two or three minutes before time runs out, and notify the team when time has expired for a topic.

- **Keeps the discussion relevant and balanced.** The team leader must make sure that the discussion is relevant, ensuring that the group does not go off on tangents or float from one point to another not on the agenda. The chair makes sure that everyone participates in the conversation. If there are any silent team members, the chair can conduct a round-robin, asking each member in turn for input on the agenda item under discussion.

- **Summarizes the proceedings after each topic.** At the conclusion of each agenda topic, the chair summarizes the discussion and the action taken.

- **Brings team to consensus, decisions, and action items.** The team leader is responsible for making sure that the group arrives at consensus, makes decisions, and determines follow-up actions. Most agenda items will require some type of decision. Depending on the team norms, decisions can be made by consensus (agreement) or vote. Action items are follow-up measures required to implement group decisions. Example action items are found in Figure 5.2 under the column heading "Action."

- **Ensures that meeting records are kept.** Written minutes of every meeting must be recorded. If a secretary has not been identified in the team charter, the chair can appoint a team member to record the minutes. To give everyone experience taking minutes, the chair can rotate this function among team members.

An example of the format and content of meeting minutes appears in Figure 5.2. Notice how the minutes follow the agenda topics in Figure 5.1. Observe that the minutes are concise but cover the details of the meeting.

Figure 5.2 Sample Meeting Minutes

Minutes: Regular Team Meeting
Date: December 1, 2006
Place: 25 East Pearson, Room 41
Present: P. Fox, J. Boomer, C. Mohle, H.Collins, B. Johnston
Absent: P. Martin

Topic	Discussion	Action
Minutes of 11/24/06	Meeting started at 7:00 pm. Minutes Reviewed	Approved
Appointment of Timekeeper and Recorder	S. Boomer: recorder C. Mohle: timekeeper	
Determine pro-ject scope	The goals of the project were reviewed and the client's desired functional-ities discussed. Given time and current resources, a limited project scope that delivered the basic func-tionalities was decided to be most feasible to purse.	Approved project scope includes development of a relational database for inventory management including screens for input, modification, and deletion of inventory items, and generation or reports.
Finalize draft diagram of current system	The draft of the diagram of the client's current system was reviewed. No correc-tions or additions to the draft.	Draft of current system diagram approved as submitted. Diagram is to be filed in team project notebook.
Finalize func-tion new system functions	Fifteen functionalities for the new system presented. P. Fox noted that security functionality was not on the list.	New system functionality was approved with the addition of security pro-tections and passwords for end user.
Determine func-tions	The list of desired func-tionalities was compared to the project scope. Six of the 15 functionalities were determined to be within the project scope.	The final list of function-alities to be delivered was approved including input, update, deletion of inventory items, and generation of reports by item number.
Assignments	Assignments were made for development of flow diagrams, entity relation-ship, and use case devel-opment.	Action item: Develop data flow diagram by 12/8 B. Johnston Action Item: Develop entity relationship by 12/8 C. Mohle Action Item: Develop use cases by 12/15 P. Fox
Action Items Next Meeting	Action items for next meet-ing include review of drafts of DFDs & ERDs.	Next meeting December 20, 2006 at Collegiate Library, Study Room 487.
Adjournment	Meeting adjourned at 9 pm	

Sometimes teams feel that minutes are burdensome to keep. But minutes are important for a high-powered team for several reasons:

- People's memories are often unreliable. Minutes provide a history of the project for future reference and review.
- Minutes not only describe the discussion but the decisions and responsibility for action items.
- Minutes help hold team members accountable for tasks.
- Minutes help avoid conflict among team members.

Role of meeting members. The responsibility for a well-run meeting does not just rest with the team leader. Team members are equally accountable and have several responsibilities for making sure that the meeting is productive. Team members' responsibilities should be defined in the team norms in the team charter. Responsibilities of team members and team leader include the following:

- **Attend meetings**. The first responsibility of team members is to attend all group meetings. Meetings are where work gets done. It is essential that every team member attend all team meetings.

- **Arrive at meetings on time**. Latecomers are disruptive to productive meetings. Arriving late at a meeting is inconsiderate to others and demonstrates a lack of discipline and commitment to the team effort.

- **Come prepared to meetings**. Unprepared team members cannot participate productively in meetings. Team members should have read the agenda for the meeting, the minutes of the previous meeting, and any reports distributed prior to the meeting. Team members should have completed all assignments at an acceptable level.

- **Follow meeting norms**. Every team member is responsible for following the team's meeting norms. When a member is in noncompliance with meeting norms, it is the responsibility of other team members to bring this to the attention of the member during the meeting and to bring the meeting back into compliance with team norms.

- **Follow meeting agenda**. Productive meetings are a result of following the prescribed meeting agenda. Getting off on tangential discussions not related to team business wastes valuable team and individual time. Team members should stick to the agenda topics. If a team member feels that an additional topic should be added for discussion, this issue should be raised with the team leader at the time the agenda is distributed. This gives the chair time to consider the appropriateness of adding the agenda item prior to the meeting and allowing sufficient time allocation to it.

- **Participate in the meeting**. Every team member is responsible for active participation in every meeting. Remaining silent on issues, withholding information, and not asking questions or seeking clarification are nonproductive behaviors. Team members are responsible for cultivating a positive meeting climate, listening and respecting other's opinions and input, and working toward achieving team goals.

Role of timekeeper. The chair appoints a meeting timekeeper. The role can rotate among team members, giving everyone an opportunity to gain experience in this role. The timekeeper's job is to make sure that the meeting stays on schedule. Approximately two to three minutes before the end of the time period allotted to an agenda item, the timekeeper makes an announcement that the time for discussion on the topic is almost finished. This allows the chair time to wrap up discussion and proceed with bringing the group to consensus or making decisions. The timekeeper announces to the group when time has expired for an agenda topic. At that point, the team leader winds up discussion on the topic.

The timekeeper can also be assigned to help the chair with the task of making sure that discussions are relevant and following the agenda. In this capacity, when discussions are going off of the agenda on a tangent, the timekeeper can remind the group of the agenda item and help direct the conversation back to the agenda item at hand.

Role of the secretary. The chair also appoints a meeting secretary (also called a recorder). The role can rotate among team members, giving everyone the opportunity to gain experience in this role.

The meeting secretary is responsible for recording the minutes of the meeting. After the meeting, the secretary types the minutes and forwards them to the chair for distribution to team members.

To ensure that minutes are accurate, the secretary should type them up no more than a day or two after the meeting. The minutes follow a prescribed format, as shown in Figure 5.2.

Evaluate Your Control Processes

Before holding your team meetings, be sure you have all the appropriate process controls in place. Use Exercise 5.1. to perform this assessment. If you answer "yes" to each item, your team has appropriate processes for conducting well-run meetings.

Exercise 5.1. Manage Meetings Productively		
Use the following checklist to make sure that your team has the appropriate process controls in place for managing meetings:	Yes	No

1. Has a team leader been identified?
 2. Have the roles of the team leader been agreed upon and written in the team charter?
 3. Have the roles of team members been agreed upon and written in the team charter?
 4. Have meeting times, place, and dates been established?
 5. Is there an established format for meeting agendas?
 6. Is there an established format for meeting minutes?
 7. Has the role of timekeeper been designated?
 8. Has the role of secretary been designated?
 9. Have team norms been established in relation to meetings, such as:
     a. Attendance rules
     b. Participation rules
     c. Rules for agendas and minutes
     d. Decision rules (how decisions are made)
     e. Preparation rules
 10. Have all team norms been written in the team charter?		

Handling Conflict

Conflict is not necessarily a bad thing! If everyone agreed on everything, progress would likely not happen. Conflict is a driving force of change. In fact, research shows that teams depend on conflict in order to thrive and prosper.

However, conflict can have a disruptive effect if it is not managed properly. Team energy, relationships, and task accomplishment can be severely damaged as a result of unmanaged conflict. Conflict will occur in meetings, and it must be well managed for the team to be productive.

When teams manage conflict, positive results occur. For example, new ideas and creative problem solving can result from managed conflict.

Handling conflict through meeting norms. Meeting norms should be part of your team's charter. If your team does not use meeting norms, it is likely to waste time, be unproductive, become negative, and have poor outcomes. Therefore, pay careful attention to developing meeting norms that address how a meeting is conducted and how participants are to behave.

Differing opinions are not conflict unless you allow disagreements to escalate. The following rules can help turn conflicting opinions into positive actions.

- **Listen to other people's opinions and concerns**. Each team member assumes responsibility for listening to the opinions of other team members. Frequently, people jump to conclusions without listening to what another person has to say. Listening also means understanding what the other person is trying to communicate. If the message is unclear, it is the team member's responsibility to ask questions in order to understand the other person's point of view.

- **Address one subject at a time.** When differences of opinion are limited to one subject or topic at a time, conflict is easier to manage. Team members are forced to focus on a particular subject, and emotion-packed issues and hidden agendas are minimized. Sticking to one agenda item at a time helps to focus team members.

- **Address facts and opinions, not personalities.** The team leader and other team members should insist that only facts and opinions about the subject at hand be addressed. Team members should not make personal remarks about other members.

- **Work toward win-win for the team.** Working toward a win-win situation for the team should be the goal of each team member. Reaching a win-win situation requires that team members do the following:
  - *Respect balance in the meeting.* Do not dominate the meeting and do not be a silent team member. Participate in discussions.
  - *Come prepared with ideas.* Be prepared to sell your ideas to the team. This means coming

prepared with information and defending your view with facts, not emotion.

- o **Relinquish an idea if it fails to receive the support of the team**. If your team gives good reasons for not supporting an idea, relinquish the idea.
- o **Evaluate the work of the team**. Provide evaluation and constructive criticism about the work of the team.
- o **Maintain positive relationships**. Maintain a supporting, respectful, and healthy relationship with all team members.
- o **Complete assignments**. Complete all tasks and assignments on time and at a high-quality level.

Review the checklist in Exercise 5.2 individually. Determine what areas you need to work on to improve conflict management on your team. Periodically use the checklist to re-evaluate how you are doing in helping your team manage conflict.

Complying with Norms and Expected Behaviors

The previous sections provide guidance for establishing norms of behavior and handling conflict. But what happens if a team member doesn't follow the norms or doesn't adopt behaviors that avoid conflict? The following section discusses methods for handling noncompliance.

Exercise 5.2.			
Individual Conflict-Management Assessment			
Use the list below and rate how well you manage conflict.			
	Always	Sometimes	Never
Attend all meetings			
Come to meetings on time			
Listen to other's opinions			
Allow others to speak without interrupting			
Ask questions during meetings to clarify			
Come to meetings with ideas			
Relinquish ideas that don't have team support			
Provide constructive criticism			
Refrain from verbal personal attacks			
Maintain positive relationships			
Complete assignments on time and at a high-quality level			

Techniques for Guiding Behaviors. One of the best ways to handle members who are not respecting team norms is to have in place techniques that check behaviors and guide them back to the desired place. The following examples illustrate this point.

> A team called the WDBA used a pencil in a technique to check monopolizing behaviors during team

meetings. At the beginning of every team meeting,
the team agreed that a pencil would be placed in
the middle of the table and when a member wanted
to speak during the meeting, he or she would pick
up the pencil. It was also agreed that if the team
member who was speaking began to monopolize
the discussion or was off the agenda, any team
member could say, "It's time to pass the pencil."
All team members agreed ahead of time that if they
were asked to "pass the pencil" they had to give up
the floor of discussion to another member.

Several qualities contribute to making this technique work. First, the approach is direct but not confrontational. No personal attacks are made; only an action is requested. Second, peer pressure is a powerful tool that guides people into compliance. In the above case, the entire team is exerting the power of peer pressure and expects that the pencil will be passed.

The next example illustrates another technique for guiding behaviors.

A team called the Buckeye Consultants used a
stuffed toy moose to address potential team con-
flict. The idea came from the common saying "No
one wants to talk about the dead moose laying in
the middle of the table." What the saying means is
that people frequently try to avoid a situation that

76

everyone knows is a problem rather than to con-
front it directly. Problems usually don't go away by
themselves. Avoidance behavior more often than
not results in extreme tension among team mem-
bers and increases rather than reduces conflict.

Buckeye Consultants decided to bring the toy
moose, Truman. to every team meeting. When any
team member had a potentially confrontational is-
sue to bring up at a team meeting, he or she would
say, "I have a Truman." The team member would
then put Truman on the table and explain the issue.
For example, the team leader might say, " I have a
Truman. This Truman involves team members be-
ing late to meetings. I want to revisit our meeting
norms to determine if our meeting time is still rea-
sonable for all team members. If it is not reason-
able, we need to change the meeting time. If it is
reasonable, we need to reconfirm our expectations
that all members will be on time to meetings."

Like the previous example, the approach is direct but not
confrontational. Notice how the team leader phrases the
issue: "This Truman involves team members being late to
meetings." This is not a personal attack; rather, it is a
statement of fact. Making statements of fact and avoiding
personal attacks form the basis for resolution of problems.
Note that the toy moose is a symbol for addressing a potential confrontational issue. It serves as surrogate or mediator

for saying, "I have something that's really bothering me or "I have a complaint." Interjecting the toy moose as the mediator lessons tensions and distances the complaint as a personal attack.

Note also in this example how the team leader goes back to the agreed-upon ground rule. The team leader allows for an option if a change in meeting time is actually warranted. However, the ground rule is still the impartial standard by which everyone is evaluated.

A third example was given in Chapter 3 in the discussion about assessing personal style. It was suggested that a good way to remember each member's dominant strength during team meetings was to make up a name card that included the strength name. The name card is then displayed for each team member during every team meeting. Knowing your team member's styles can help reduce conflict.

Usually I have found that teams using a direct approach to a situation have good success in remedying it. A direct approach is different than a confrontational approach. A direct approach addresses the facts of a situation, uses a problem solving technique and looks at a situation objectively, without emotional drama. The following example illustrates a direct approach to a potentially confrontational situation.

A student team called Marketing Dynamics was doing a marketing analysis project for a small downtown business district as a project assignment. One of the tasks was to interview eight small retail business owners in the district. One team member, Marco, was assigned the interviewing task. At the weekly team meetings it was evident that interviews were not being conducted on a timely basis and were off schedule. Not having interview results on schedule would put the whole team in jeopardy of not completing the class project on time. The team leader addressed the situation in a direct manner during a team meeting with the following statement: "Our team is not meeting its scheduled timeline in completing the business interviews. We need to find out why this is happening and how we can rectify it if we are to complete the class project on time. Marco, please tell us your perspective on why this task is off schedule."

Notice that the team leader keeps the conversation direct but not personal. The language the leader uses states the fact that the interviews are off schedule and lets everyone know what the ramifications are for the team. The team leader does not accuse Marco of not doing his job; rather, the team leader gives Marco an opportunity to explain what has happened.

In examining the situation, the team found that the interview for each business was taking double the time that had been originally anticipated. Therefore, Marco was behind in his interviews. To rectify this problem, the remaining businesses to be interviewed were divided between Marco and two other team members. This put the team back on schedule for completing the project.

You can see that a different outcome could have resulted had the team members jumped to the conclusion that Marco was a "social loafer" rather than the positive outcome that resulted using a direct problem-solving approach.

Using these examples as guides, your team should always opt to solve problems directly in a problem-solving rather than a confrontational manner. However, there still may be times when someone on the team just does not want to conform to the team behavior norms. Three strategies to handled this situation are discussed below.

Using documentation. The power of the team in ensuring equitable treatment in final grade assignments is in its documentation and evaluation materials. In your project notebook, you are documenting how the project is being carried out. All team members should be clear that the project notebook serves as a device for the instructor to track and monitor individual team member contributions to the final product and ultimately to the individual's grade on the course project.

For example, when team members are late to meetings, the team should document this in the team minutes. In reviewing the team minutes, your instructor can see who came late to meetings and how often this occurred. If a team member does not turn in assignments on time, document this in the team minutes as well as the weekly interim team reports. If a team member submits sub-quality work, document this in the weekly interim team reports. In reviewing these reports, your instructor will see who has and who hasn't turned in assignments on time or at expected quality levels.

In addition to the regular team reports such as minutes and interim reports, your team should complete individual evaluations at the end of the course. This gives each team member an opportunity to evaluate every other team member on several objective measures. (An example of such an evaluation is found in Chapter 9.) Individual team evaluations are turned into the instructor at the end of the course and used to evaluate how team members contributed to the course project.

In rare cases, having ground rules and using conflict-management techniques and evaluation mechanisms may still fail to thwart a disruptive team member. In these cases, the course instructor must be made aware of the situation and be the final arbitrator and decision maker on what course of action is necessary.

Meetings Evaluation

To help make sure that your team meetings are productive and are following good meeting procedure, at the conclusion of each meeting your team should evaluate the meeting. Use Appendix C to help you perform this evaluation.

If your evaluation shows that the meeting processes are not being followed, the team needs to assess the underlying causes for this and take corrective action. For example, if the meeting is not starting on time, why is this the case? Does the meeting time need to be changed? If the meeting is not ending on time, is this an agenda or a facilitation problem? The goals should be to always conduct productive, efficient meetings. All meeting evaluations should be filed in the team's project notebook.

Exercise 5.3. Add to the Team's Project Notebook

Your team should have developed a project notebook as part of Exercise 3.3 in Chapter 3.

Using Appendix B as a guide, add copies of the team checklist for process control to the team's project notebook.

Summary

Well-run meetings result in efficient use of time, good decision making, positive outcomes, and a high level of team camaraderie. If the team follows good process controls and meeting behavior norms, good meetings will result.

Good meeting process include skilled facilitation and focus on agenda items. The team leader functions as the meeting chair and takes charge of meeting proceedings. Team members are responsible for attending and coming prepared to meetings. The meeting timekeeper is responsible for making sure the meeting schedule is followed. The secretary records well-written minutes. All team members are responsible for complying with meeting and conflict-resolution norms.

Items used for evaluating how well the team manages meetings include the following:

- Team checklist of meeting process controls
- Individual assessment of conflict management behaviors
- Meeting evaluations (See Appendix C).

Chapter 6
Defining the Project

*If project content is allowed to change freely, the rate of
change will exceed the rate of progress.*
(Mark Harding Roberts)

 Once your team has solidi-
fied its team belief and estab-
lished the first elements of its
charter, it is time to move on
to defining the requirements
of your course project.   Before beginning the course project, your team members must agree on its scope, objectives, and outcomes.   This chapter describes the contents
of a project-definition document and how your team can go
about defining your project.

Project-Definition Document

A project-definition document describes the common understanding among team members and the instructor (and client if this is a simulation) about the nature of the project.
The project definition becomes a part of the team charter
and serves as a contract between the team members (and
client), clearly stating expectations for project scope, timeline, resources, and results. Developing a project definition
in the beginning will save your team time in the long run.
Teams that do not write a clear project definition usually

wind up making changes throughout the project that waste time, causing frustration and disagreement among team members.

The team develops the project-definition document together. Your course instructor will provide you with an outline or description of the project. You will use this information to create the project definition.

Several components make up the project-definition document:

1. **Problem statement**. Briefly (a few sentences) describe the problem to be addressed and resolved. For example, let's say that your instructor has given you a sample of a marketing plan for a small retail business and asks you to evaluate the plan. Your team might come up with the following problem statement:

   Given a marketing plan for a small retail business, assess the plan's strengths and weaknesses, considering the business goals and market niche, competition, target audience, and allocated marketing budget.

   Notice that the problem definition defines the problem to be solved. The problem definition guides the team in the work that it must do.

In this example, the problem definition determines the team has to do several things. The team will have to evaluate the marketing plan relative to the goals of the sample retail business, the competition, and the market niche and target audience. To do this, the team must find out the goals of the business, determine the competition, and assess the market niche and who the target audience includes. After completing these tasks, the team can then assess the strengths and weaknesses of the marketing plan.

In most cases, the problem definition is stated in the course assignment the instructor provides. However, the statement may be worded in general terms. Such as "Develop sample policies and procedures for managing a call center." Therefore, it is extremely important that the team come to agreement on the details of the problem statement so that every team member understands exactly the project outcome and what work it will take to achieve it.

2. **Project name**. The name should describe the project. For example, if the team is working on developing a sales database application for a used car dealership, the project name might be "Triple A Used Cars Sales Database."

3. **Project description**. The description includes two sections:

   - The project's background
   - The project's current status

   In a business-related course in a project assessing a small retail business marketing plan, for example, the background could include information about the history of the company or stakeholders, a description of the current environment, a list of the significant stakeholders, a description of the physical facilities, names of employees, and other resources.

   The current project status is a description of the current operation of the project, perceived deficiencies, and desired improvements. In the example above, the current status might include a description of how marketing is currently being done, and a discussion of perceived deficiencies in the current process, and any desired improvements.

4. **Project scope**. Many student projects fail because of something called "scope creep." The quote at the beginning of this chapter alludes to this problem. Scope creep happens when the project continually grows because more and more work is added to it. Sometimes this is referred to as a "runaway project." If project boundaries are not set at the beginning, your team runs the risk of a runaway

project. As more and more work is added to the
project, team tensions run high, adding to team
frustration and conflict, and ultimately resulting in
the team not finishing the project on time.

Therefore, your team must identify the scope of the
project and state what will and *will not* be included
in the final deliverable or product.

The case study at the end of this chapter is an example of how one student team kept its project
scope within reasonable boundaries.

5. **Project constraints**. Every project has limits to
    what can reasonably be done. For example, time,
    money, and people resources are common ele-
    ments that can constrain or restrict a project. Pro-
    ject constraints that your team may consider include
    the time you have to complete your assignment
    (usually this is an academic quarter or semester),
    the skills of the team's members, and the resources
    available to you. Understanding the constraints will
    help you establish the boundaries and scope of
    your project.

6. **Project objectives**. Project objectives are the spe-
    cifics of what the team will achieve and deliver as
    the final project. Using the marketing plan evalua-

tion above as an example, project objectives might
include the following:

- Determine the market niche
- Identify the top 10 competitors within a 25-mile radius of the business
- Identify the marketing strategies of the top five competitors
- Determine the target market
- Determine the best media mix to reach the target market

Notice that these objectives are specific and list the
products to be produced. Project objectives are
explored more in the case study at the end of this
chapter.

7. **Estimated timeline**: All projects have a start date
   and an end date. In a classroom environment, the
   project start and end dates are usually included in
   the syllabus. The estimated timeline includes a
   task list and identifies responsibilities for completion.

8. **Costs**. All projects involve some type of costs. In
   the classroom setting, costs might include such
   things as copying costs and office supply costs.
   Because costs for the completion of the course project should be equitably distributed, your team

should estimate what these costs might be and include them in your project description.

9. **Resources required**. Projects usually require a number of resources. For example, in a class project, resources might include access to computer software, computers, meeting space, reference books and materials, and so on. Identifying required resources at the project beginning is important and helps to ensure that your team has the right materials when they need them.

10. **Project leader/oversight**: The final component of the project definition is the name and contact information of the team leader, who provides oversight for the entire project.

Case Study

The case study beginning on the next page leads you through the process of developing a project-definition document. Read through the case study. Then review the project-definition document that follows it. Notice that all the components discussed above are included in the definition document. Also notice how each component is written and the overall format of the document.

A junior-level systems analysis college class was assigned a team project to develop a computer database for a real-world client who owned a used car dealership.

The following project parameters were provided by the course instructor in the course syllabus:

- Develop a working computer relational database that meets the identified needs of the client and whose scope is appropriate given time and resource constraints of the class.
- Deliver a team project history notebook to the instructor that includes all project documentation, including project definition document, time schedules, interim project reports, technical charts, meeting agendas and minutes, and evaluations.
- Provide the instructor and the client with a written final report that includes project objectives, project scope, description of current system, description of new system, listing of functions of the new computer database, summary of the new computer database, and user manual.
- The project deliverables are due on the last course session of the semester.

The student team consisted of five students. Before the team developed a project-definition document, they met with the client to determine the client's needs and to establish the scope of the project given time and other constraints.

After meeting with the client, the team identified the following client needs:

- Automate all forms used by the dealership
- Provide an up-to-date daily computer inventory of all vehicles on the lot
- Create weekly reports that include profit margin, origin of cars, list of cars sold each month, cars available, basic car information, and salesperson performance
- Track all vehicle expenses, such as costs for all repairs and all parts purchased

In addition to collecting the above information, the student team also studied the client's current paper system, including reviewing all paper forms and all manual processes. Armed with all of this information, the team was ready to develop their project definition.

The team's project-definition document appears in Figure 6.1. (The general format guidelines appear in Figure 6.2.)

Notice that all of the elements of a project definition are included in the document in Figure 6.1. The project description briefly provides the background and current status of operations. Observe what is included in the project scope and that the student team is very specific in stating what will be included and what will be excluded from the project scope. Although the client had asked for more functionality, the student team narrowed the project scope to what was achievable within the semester time frame.

The team has listed the project constraints. Principally, these include time and the type of software that is going to be used for the project. The project objectives are specific statements that elaborate on the project scope. The project definition document finishes with a statement of timeline, project costs, and the required resources to get the project done. Finally, the document ends with the team leader's contact information.

Figure 6.1. Sample Project Definition

Project Definition Document

Date Prepared: September 7, 2006

Project Name: Triple A Used Car Dealership Database

Project Members: J. Barnes K. Davis, O. Holms, M. Prentice, J.O'Rafferty

Project Description:

Background: Triple A is a used car dealership. The company has six employees. The company acquires used vehicles at auction, from other dealers, or from trade-ins. There are approximately 50 vehicles at any time on the company's car lot. Currently all information about vehicle acquisition, inventory, repair, and sales is gathered and maintained through manual and paper processes.

Current status: Manual processing of forms frequently leads to inaccuracies and is inefficient. The company wants to automate all of its forms and its processes for tracking inventory, vehicle expense, customers, and salesperson performance. The company wants to automate reports on cars sold each month, cars available on hand, basic car information, and salesperson performance. There are three personal computers with a DSL connection. Each computer is equipped with the Windows 2000 operating system. The company has a laser jet printer/copy/fax machine.

Project Scope:

The project scope will focus on automation of:

1. The Bill of Sale and the Sales Tax Transaction forms
2. Inventory system for tracking all vehicles on the car lot at any given time
3. Reports to include monthly report on car sold, daily reports of cars available on hand, and reports of individual car basic information.

Functionalities that will not be addressed in this phase of the project include: Vehicle expense tracking and salesperson performance tracking.

Project Constraints:

The project is to be completed in eight weeks. The software used for development is Microsoft Access 2000.

Project Objectives:

1. Deliver a relational database that tracks car inventory and basic car information
2. Provide end user interface to automate data entry for the Bill of Sale and Sales Tax Transaction forms, car inventory, and car basic information
3. Implement search features for searching any data item within the car inventory system
4. Generate automatic reports from the car inventory database that provides monthly reports of cars sold and daily reports of cars available and basic car information on current inventory.

Project Timeline

Project start date is September 15, 2006. Project end date is December 1. 2006.

Project Costs

Project costs include office supplies and printing amounting to 73.00

Required Resources

Personal computers with Windows Operating System. MicroSoft Access 2000 relational database software.

Team Leader: Janice Barnes. Ph: 815-220-9000.

Exercise 6.2.   Add to the Team Project Notebook

Your team should have developed a project notebook as part of Exercise 3.3 in Chapter 3.

Using Appendix B as a guide, add a copy of the project-definition document to the team project notebook. Use the template in Figure 6.2 and develop your project definition.

Figure 6.2. Project-Definition Document Template

Project-Definition Document
Date prepared: Project name: Project members: Project description: Project scope: Project constraints: Project objectives: Project timeline: Project costs: Required resources: Team leader:

Summary

A project-definition document describes the common under-standing among team members, instructor (and client if this is a simulation) of the nature of the project. The project definition becomes a part of the team charter and serves as a contract between the team members (and client), clearly stating expectations for project scope, timeline, resources, and results.

Developing a project definition in the beginning saves your team time in the long run because it sets out the basic roadmap of what the project is and where it is going.

Teams that write a clear project definition usually make fewer changes during the project than those who do not have a project-definition document. Furthermore, those teams that have a well-written project definition use their time more efficiently and ultimately are more productive.

Once the team has defined the project, it can move on to planning in detail how to conduct the project. The next chapter leads you through the planning process.

Chapter 7
Planning the Project

If you fail to plan, you are planning to fail.
(Mike Harding Roberts)

 To complete the course project, your team must put together a plan of action. This is referred to as project planning. Your plan of action must consider what tasks need to be completed, the resources required to complete each task, and how information and communication will be exchanged among team members and other stakeholders. Planning your team project requires that your team answer the following questions:

- What tasks need to be completed?
- In what order must the tasks be completed?
- How long will it take to complete each task?
- Who is responsible for completing each task?
- What resources are required to complete each task?
- How is information communicated among team members and other stakeholders?

This chapter explores each of these questions and includes exercises to help your team plan your project.

Develop Project Task List

Developing a task list is the first step in project planning. The task list is the roadmap for the action plan. Once your team prepares the list, analyze each task and determine how long it should take to complete and if its completion depends on other tasks being completed before it. Then identify what resources are required to accomplish each task.

It is usually easier to develop your task list by first identifying categories of tasks that need to be done. For example, if your team is working on developing a database application like the one in the case study in Chapter 6, the categories of tasks might include the following:

- System analysis tasks
- System design tasks
- System development tasks

Once you have identified the main categories, you can list more specific tasks within each category. Continuing with the above example, more specific tasks within the systems analysis category might include:

1. Conduct an initial client meeting.
2. Review the current system.
3. Hold a joint application development meeting.
4. Compile a report of the joint application development meeting.
5. Develop data flow diagrams of the current system.

6. Develop data flow diagrams of the new system.
7. Meet with the client to confirm functionalities of the new system.
8. Determine functions to be incorporated into the first prototype design.

Once you have identified all of the tasks within each category, be sure to arrange them in the order in which they should be performed (as in the list above).

Develop task time frames

Once the team has identified tasks and put them in a logical sequence for completion, assign start and end dates to each. A Gantt chart, such as that in Figure 7.1, is usually used to plot the tasks and their time frames, and to identify who is responsible for completing each task.

Software programs such as Microsoft Project, Eproject, and Basecamp are used to create Gantt, PERT, and similar charts for tracking tasks. If your team does not have access to these software programs, you can easily develop a Gantt chart using a word-processing program and designing the chart using the table application.

The sample Gantt chart in Figure 7.1 was developed in Microsoft Project while the one in Figure 7.2 was developed using a word-processing application. Notice how the student team has broken the tasks into categories. Each task is given an identification number. Each task is assigned a start and an end date, and a team member has been assigned responsibility for completion of each task.

Figure 7.1. Gantt Chart Using Microsoft Project

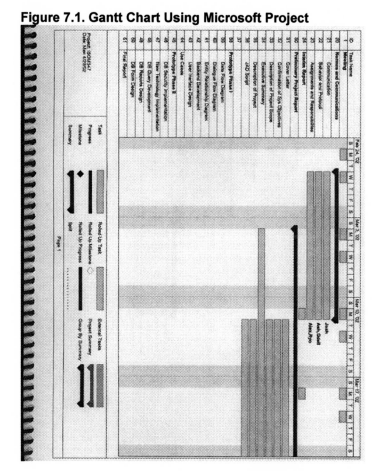

99

Figure 7.2 Gantt Chart Using a Word-Processing Program

ID	Task	Feb 24, 02							Mar 03, 02							Mar 10, 02							Mar 17, 02						
		S	M	T	W	T	F	S	S	M	T	W	T	F	S	S	M	T	W	T	F	S	S	M	T	W	T	F	S
1	Meetings																												
20	Norms/Communications				J																								
21	Communication				AH	O																							
22	Behavior/Protocol				AX	R																							
23	Assignments																												
24	Interim Reports																												
30	Preliminary Report																												
31	Cover Letter																												
32	Sys Objectives																												
33	Project Scope																												
34	Executive Summary																												
35	Project Description																												
36	JAD Script																												
38	Prototype Phase I																												
39	Data Flow Diagram																												
40	Dialog Flow Diagram																												
41	Entity Rel Diagram																												
42	Backend Development																												
43	User Interface Design																												
44	Use Cases																												
45	Prototype Phase II																												
46	DB Security																												
47	Tech Implementation																												
48	DB Query Development																												
48	DB Reports Design																												
50	DB Form Design																												
51	Final Report																												

Responsibilities: J=Josh, AH = Ash, O = Odell, AX = Alex, R = Ryo

Note: Starting and ending dates for Prototype Phase I and Prototype Phase II are located on the second sheet of both Gantt charts and are not shown in the above diagrams.

Exercise 7.1. Develop Task List and Gantt Chart

Brainstorm with your team members to determine the categories of tasks required to complete the course project. For each category, identify the specific tasks that must be completed. List these tasks in the sequence they should be performed. Some tasks may overlap or may be completed in parallel.

After the task list is complete, assign start and end dates for each task.

Using a project management software program or a word-processing program, construct a Gantt chart. List the tasks by category in the first column of the chart. In the top row of the chart, construct a weekly timeline. Use a line or bar to indicate the start and end times for each task on the appropriate row.

Assign task responsibility

Assigning the right person to the right task is one of the standards for a high-powered team. This means that tasks are matched to the skills and interests of the team members. Remember, this is a course project. The purpose of course projects is to build the skill level of each student. One way to increase skill levels is to match an "expert" student with a "novice" student to work on the same task. In this way, the novice can learn from the expert, and the expert can improve her or his skills by teaching the novice.

It is important to balance task assignments in the student team. One or two students in the group should not be completing the majority of the project work. The purpose of the course project is to increase the skills of all team members.

101

It is the responsibility of all team members to make sure that everyone contributes equally to the final product.

The team needs to review each task and determine what skills are necessary to complete it. Then the team identifies team members who:

- Have the skills to perform the task
- Have an interest in performing the task
- Want to increase their skill level by performing the task

Through consensus, the team matches team members and tasks. Use Exercise 7.2 to assign responsibility for task completion to team members.

Exercise 7.2.   Assign Task Responsibilities

Using the Task-Assignment Grid in Figure 7.3 as a model, assign team members responsibility for completing project tasks.

List your project tasks on the task-assignment grid. Review each task and identify the skills required to carry out the task.

For each task, identify team members who:
- Have the skills to perform the task,
- Have an interest in performing the tasks
- Want to increase their skill level by performing the task.

By consensus, assign responsibility for each task to one or more team members. Add responsibilities for each task to the team's Gantt chart.

Figure 7.3 Task-Assignment Grid

Task and Skills	Has Skills	Has Interest	Build Skills	Final Assignment
#39 Develop Data Flow Diagram Skills: Case Tools	J	J, O	O	J, O
#40 Dialog Flow Diagram Skills: Visio Software	AS	AS, AX	AX, R	AS, AX, R
#41 Entity Relationship Diagrams Skills: Case Tools	J	J, O, AS, AX	AS, AX, R	J, AS, AX
#42 Backend Development	J, AS	O	O	AS, O

Team Members: J= Josh, AS= Ash, O= Odell, AX = Alex, R = Ryo

Using the Gantt Chart

The Gantt chart lists your team's tasks, timelines, and re-sponsibilities. It is important that your team refers to and uses the Gantt chart throughout the course of the entire project. All of the planning in the world will not help if you leave your plan in a binder or folder and never refer to it.

Use your Gantt chart for schedule management. At each team meeting, compare your actual work progress to the schedule in the Gantt chart. Assess if your team is staying on schedule. If you are off schedule, you will need to ad-dress the ramifications of not completing tasks on time. In Chapter 8, Managing the Project, these issues are studied in more detail.

Identify Project Resources and Costs

Besides people and time, projects require other resources that need to be taken into account for planning purposes.

These may include resources such as facilities, meeting rooms, computers, software programs, and office supplies and other materials.

Figure 7.4 shows how a student team listed the resources needed to complete each task. Notice that the team indicated where the resources are located and identified their associated costs. You can see that planning of this kind contributes to a smoother functioning team by preventing confusion and emergencies.

Figure 7.4. Task-Resource Requirements List

Task Resource Requirements		
Task	Availability	Costs
#39 Data Flow Diagram Resources		
Case Tools	Available in CIS Computer Lab	None
#40 Dialog Flow Diagram Resources		
Case Tools	Available in CIS Computer Lab	None
#42 Backend Development Resources		
Microsoft Access Application	Available in CIS, MIS Computer Lab	None
#47 Project Tracking		
Basecamp Project Software	Internet	Free Trial
#72 Project Report		
Copying and Binding of Report. 1 copy per team member; 1 copy for instructor	Copy Express	$7.00 per team member

Use Exercise 7.3. to help your team identify any additional resources needed to complete your project.

Exercise 7.3.   List Project Resources and Costs

Use Figure 7.4 as a model for outlining task-resource requirements.

Reviewing your project task list, determine what resources are required to complete each task. List these resources and where they can be obtained; for example, software programs may be available in specific computer labs. Meeting rooms may be available in the library. Some resources may be available from team members.

Determine any associated costs that the team will have to incur for each of the listed resources, for example, copying charges and fees for binding the final project. Determine how these costs will be divided among group members and how payment will be made.

Develop a Communication Plan

Once you have considered project resources, identified your tasks and timelines, and assigned responsibilities, your team is ready to develop its communication plan.

A communication plan is an integral part of project planning. The plan identifies how communication is exchanged within your team and to other stakeholders. A communication plan ensures that all parties who need to be informed about project activities and results get the information they need.

The communication plan identifies stakeholders, their communication needs, and how information will be communicated to them. Stakeholders in a real-world project may include team members, managers, clients, departments, and other teams. In a course project, the major stakeholders usually include team members, the instructor, other course teams or students in the course, and perhaps a client.

The course requirements given in your course syllabus may stipulate how communication will occur between your team and the instructor, for example, through weekly written status reports. Course requirements may also specify how communication will occur between the team and other class members, for example, through oral presentations.

Your team needs to specify how it will handle communication internally. Will your team use e-mail as a primary medium to transfer information or an Internet project management/tracking application? What are the expectations for checking e-mail and/or message boards? Should e-mail be checked every day, including weekends, for project information and updates? You may have already listed some of these expectations in the communication norms in your team charter.

However, the communication plan is broader than communication within the team. The communication plan also includes the following:

- **Project stakeholders**. Who are the stakeholders?
- **Stakeholder information needs**. What type of information does each stakeholder need? For example, some stakeholders may need regular status reports; others may require review of project deliverables.

- **Communication methods**. How will information be communicated to each of the stakeholders? Some possibilities are formal written project status reports, oral presentations, e-mail updates, and meetings.

Figure 7.5 shows an example of a student team's communication plan. Notice that the team has identified the project stakeholders, their information needs, and how communication will be handled. The team has also included its communication norms as part of the plan.

Figure 7.5 Team Communication Plan

Project Name: Triple A Used Car Dealership Database			
Stakeholder	Information Needs	Communication Type	Frequency
Team Members	Project Task Status	Team Meetings	Weekly
	Agendas, Minutes	Web board	Weekly
	Collaborative Work Update	Web bulletin board	Daily
Class Members	Progress Report	Oral Class Presentation	Mid and end semester
Client	Progress Reports	Meeting	Every two weeks
Instructor	Interim Reports	Paper Report	Weekly

Communication Norms:
- Team meetings are held each Wednesday evening from 6:00 – 8:00 pm.
- The team web bulletin board is used as the primary means of communication among team members.
- Web bulletin board messages are checked by all team members on a daily basis, excluding Sundays.
- All agendas and minutes of team meetings are posted to the team web bulletin board.
- All interim and other reports are posted to the team web bulletin board.
- All work materials are posted to the team web bulletin board.

Use Exercise 7.4 to develop your team's communication plan. Once it has been completed, every team member should receive a copy. The communication plan should be put in the team's project notebook.

Exercise 7.4.   Develop a Communication Plan
Make a list of project stakeholders. Identify the type of information each stakeholder needs and the frequency of its distribution.

For each stakeholder and type of information required, identify how information will be distributed. Identify who on the team will be responsible for communication of information to the various stakeholders. In some cases, the entire team may be responsible for an oral presentation or a meeting with a client.

Exercise 7.4 Add to the Team Project Notebook
Your team should have developed a project notebook as part of Exercise 3.3 in Chapter 3.

Using Appendix B as a guide, add the following to the team project notebook: Gantt chart, task assignment grid, task resource requirements list, and communication plan.

Summary

In this chapter, you have learned the essential elements of planning your course project. Actions that are important for project planning include:

- Developing a task list
- Determining start and end dates for each task
- Matching team member skills to tasks
- Assigning task responsibility
- Developing a Gantt chart

- Determining resources needed
- Determining project costs
- Developing a communication plan

Chapter 8
Managing the Project

All project managers face problems on Monday mornings--
good project managers work on next Monday's problems.
(Mike Harding Roberts)

 Once you have planned your project, it is time to take action and move forward. Tracking your team's progress in meeting your project's goals, schedule, and costs, and ensuring that required resources are available are all part of managing the project.

This chapter guides you through the steps your team must take to manage the project and to make sure that plans are turned into action.

Hold Team Meetings

How does a team assess whether goals are being met and tasks are being completed on schedule? Interim team meetings are the usual way teams manage their projects. Meetings are held to assess task status and completion, and scheduling and resource needs. Team meetings also serve to identify problems in meeting project schedule or task completion and to readjust the project plan if needed. You should hold meetings at least weekly, but hold them more often if necessary.

Interim meetings provide an opportunity for the entire team to get together, share information, and collectively assess project status, make decisions, and solve problems. Interim meetings should include:

- Reviewing project status
- Communicating each member's progress in meeting assignments
- Determining percentage of completion of each project task
- Identifying potential problems and how these may affect project schedule, resources, or costs
- Determining solutions to problems affecting the project
- Making changes to the project plan if required
- Sharing information from external stakeholders.

Prepare Interim Reports

You should compile a written report for each interim team meeting. The reports show which team members have been responsible for tasks during the past period and what the workload of team members will be for the upcoming period. In this way, the interim report holds team members accountable for their work.

Reports are compiled in a specific format and distributed to the course instructor and members of the team. Usually the team leader is responsible for compiling and distributing the interim reports. A copy of all interim reports is maintained in the project notebook. Interim reports *do not* take the place of meeting minutes. Figure 8.1 shows a sample team interim report.

Figure 8.1. Sample Interim Project Report

Project Name:	Triple A Car Dealership
Interim Report Date:	11/22/06
Prepared By:	Janet Barns, Team Leader SMT Consultants

Accomplishments to Date:
1. Team name has been created
2. Communication plan developed and contact information exchanged among team members
3. Team agreed that email is the primary means of communication
4. Meeting days will be Monday, Wednesday, Sunday 4:00 – 5:30 pm
5. Project charter has been created
6. Gantt chart has been created
7. Project definition has been created
8. Meeting with client has been conducted

Project Milestones Not Met:
All milestones have been met. Project is on schedule.

Task Assignments completed this week:
Interim report completed – J. Barnes
Team has completed project Charter – group effort
Team conducted meeting with client – group effort

Task Assignments scheduled but not completed this week
Minutes from last meeting were not done by K. Davis. K. Davis has been asked to have these prepared as per meeting norms.

Assignments for next period:
Minutes – A. Varner
Description of functionality of new system – J. Barnes
Narrative of current system – K. Davis
Data flow diagram of current system – O. Holmes

Notice that the first part of the report includes a running list of the team's accomplishments to date. The team lists all the tasks completed since its last interim report and lists what tasks were assigned but not completed. (In this example, one team member did not complete his task.) Listing completed and non-completed tasks in this way documents who has performed work and who hasn't. This type of

112

documentation is important for giving credit to appropriate team members when final project grades are assigned.

From this example, you can see how interim reports are essential in documenting how a team has managed a project. Taken as a whole, the team and instructor can review the interim reports and assess the degree to which the team stayed on schedule, whether there was an equitable workload among team members, and how well team members met deadlines. This assessment is important, particularly in evaluating each team participant and assigning individual final grades for the project work.

Your team should use the interim reports to assess the following:

- Is your team staying on schedule?
- If the team is not on schedule, what is the underlying cause? How will the team make adjustments and correct the problem so that it does not occur again?
- Is each team member completing tasks as assigned and on time?
- Is the task load for each member equitable? If someone is doing too much or too little, how does the team plan to handle this inequity?
- Are task loads assigned reasonable?
- If task loads are not reasonable, how does the team plan to make adjustments?

Your team should make these assessments regularly during the project as well as at the end of the project. Use the team-assessment instrument in Appendix D to help you with this task.

All project interim reports are filed in the project notebook.

Using Figure 8.1.as a guide, prepare team interim reports.

Exercise 8.1. Prepare Interim Reports

Unless otherwise directed by your instructor, interim reports should be developed weekly. The interim reports should contain the following information:

- Date of report
- Project name
- Name of individual preparing the report
- Accomplishments to date: This is a running total of all tasks completed.
- Project milestones not met: This includes a list of tasks scheduled for completion during this period that are off-schedule.
- Task assignments completed this period: List of tasks completed during this period and what team member completed them.
- Task assignments not completed: List of task assignments scheduled but not completed this period and name of team member responsible for the task.
- Assignments next period: List of tasks for the next period and name of team member responsible for completion.

Copies of the interim report are distributed to all team members, the instructor, and other interested stakeholders. A copy of each interim report is to be maintained in the project notebook.

Use the model of an interim report in Figure 8.1 to develop your own interim reports.

Exercise 8.2. Add to the Team Project Notebook

Your team should have developed a project notebook as part of Exercise 3.3 in Chapter 3.

Using Appendix B as a guide, add the team's interim reports to your project notebook.

Summary

The team meeting is the principal tool used to manage the project. During team meetings, you review project status, details on task completion, and how the project is meeting schedule and cost constraints. If necessary, your team makes decisions about readjusting the project schedule or project resources. The team leader is responsible for writing interim weekly reports that include information on completion of tasks, outstanding tasks, and new team assignments. A copy of the interim project report is usually given to the course instructor and each team member, and a copy is filed in the project notebook.

Chapter 9
Project Closeout

 Hooray! Your team has completed its project. Because the team has adhered to the standards of a high-powered team, the experience has been enjoyable and educational for everyone. But you're not quite finished. The team still has a number of activities to perform. This phase of the project is normally called project closeout. These activities tie up the loose ends in a project and provide final documentation to the instructor and the client, if there has been one. This chapter guides you through these activities.

Hold Final Client Meeting

If the course project involved working with a client, your team will hold a final client meeting. The team gives the client a final project report along with the project deliverable. The following is a list of the usual contents of the final project report to the client:

- Cover letter thanking the client for choosing your "firm" and outlining the contents of the report

- Executive summary of the project definition, background, scope, work completed, and description of deliverable

- Details of work completed, schedule, costs. and description of the deliverable

- Appendices, which may include original contract or proposal, diagrams, flow charts, and other supporting documentation

- A sign-off form or checklist is provided to the client for signature. The sign-off form verifies that all work has been completed according to the original proposal or contract with the client.

Prepare Final Project Report

Your team is responsible for preparing a final project report and distributing it to all team members and to the course instructor. The final report content depends on the type of project your team completed. For example, in the database example used in the case study in Chapter 6, students were required to provide a formal written report to the client and the course instructor. For most teams in that class, the report was approximately 50 pages long and included the following:

- Cover letter

- Table of contents

- Executive summary

- List of system objectives

- Statement of project scope and constraints

- Narrative of the current system, with diagrams

- Narrative of the new system, with diagrams

- Functionality of the new system database

- Relational data model

- Working database application

- User manual

- Appendices

For your final project report, your course instructor should provide an outline of content and the required report format.

Conduct Post-Project Evaluation

As a final step in closing out your project, your team should perform a post-project evaluation, sometimes called a project retrospective or post-mortem review. This review is performed to identify how well your team did in planning and executing the project. A major purpose of the course project is to develop both team and technical skills. Evaluations of what went well, what did not go well, and how project teamwork could be improved are addressed in the post-project evaluation. Your team should use this evaluation as an opportunity to fully assess team skills and how these might be improved.

Recall that Chapter 1 discussed that job applicants are increasingly being asked about their team experience and how they can demonstrate that they are team players. Questions similar to those below are often used during job interviews. Use these questions to reflect on your experience in this team. Then use the form in Figure 9.1 to perform a team-process evaluation. Complete this evaluation together, not individually. Give a copy of the evaluation to each team member and to the course instructor.

- Give an example of a successful project you were part of. What was your role? Why was the project successful?

- Describe two situations from your past work experience in which you have determined a team was the best potential solution to a problem, a needed process improvement, or a planned change. How did each work out?

- What actions and support, in your experience, make a team function successfully?

- Give an example of a time when your work group or department worked especially well with another work group or department to accomplish a goal.

- Have you been a member of a team that struggled or failed to accomplish its goal? If so, what assessment did you make of the reasons for the failure?

Exercise 9.1. Perform post-project evaluation
Using the form in figure 9.1 as a model, evaluate your team process. Identify areas of strength and weaknesses. Suggest ways that your process could be improved.

Figure 9.1 Team Post-Project Evaluation

Date:
Team Name:
Team Members:

Team Organization: On a scale of 1 to 10 with 10 being the highest, how well did the team manage its activities? Was the team well organized? Did the team use all the process controls explained in this manual to organize the team? To what degree was there overall commitment to delivering the best product and "doing what it takes" to get the job done?

Strengths:

Weaknesses:

Suggested improvements:

Meetings and Communications: How well were meetings organized and run? Was the team able to reach consensus and make decisions?

Strengths:

Weaknesses:

Suggested improvements:

Project Definition, Planning & Management: How well was the project defined? Were there problems in the scope or project definition? How well was the project managed? Was the timeline realistic? Were tasks completed on time and of an acceptable quality?

Strengths:

Weaknesses:

Suggested improvements:

Team Synergy: How well did team members work together? Were team members able to give and receive feedback from each other? How well was conflict managed?

Strengths:

Weaknesses:

Suggested improvements:

Perform Individual Team Evaluations

Each team member should evaluate the contributions of every other team member, by using an evaluation form such as the example in Figure 9.2.

Copies of the evaluation for each team member should be given to the course instructor and to the individual team member being evaluated. The evaluation has several purposes. First it provides feedback to the individual team member. This feedback is useful for helping team members assess their interpersonal, technical, and team skills. Second the evaluation is useful in helping the instructor assign an individual grade for project work to each team member.

In completing the individual evaluation, you need to be sure that your assessment is backed up by evidence. This is where the project history notebook can play an important role. For example, if you rate a team member low in attending team meetings, your evaluation should be backed up by the copies of the minutes in the project notebook. The minutes should show that the team member was frequently absent at team meetings. Or if you rate a team member high in being counted on to finish tasks, then the interim project reports should back up your assessment by showing that the team member always completed her or his tasks on time.

Exercise 9.2. Individual Team Evaluations

Using the form provided in Figure 9.2. or another form provided by your instructor, evaluate the contribution and teamwork of each team member.

Figure 9.2. Team Member Evaluation

Individual Team Evaluation

Team Member Evaluated: _____

Evaluated by: _____

Place an X in the bracket closest to the statement that is the best description of the team member's contribution, participation, and activities on the team.

1. Could be counted on to be present at all team meetings	( ) ( ) ( ) ( ) ( ) ( )	Was not always on time or present at all team meetings
2. Shares opinions with team freely	( ) ( ) ( ) ( ) ( ) ( )	Usually withholds opinions unless team asks
3. Is likely to be impartial during team conflict	( ) ( ) ( ) ( ) ( ) ( )	Is likely to take one side during team conflict
4. Accepts constructive criticism	( ) ( ) ( ) ( ) ( ) ( )	Resists criticism and team input
5. Generates ideas for the team	( ) ( ) ( ) ( ) ( ) ( )	Relies on other to generate ideas
6. Can be counted on to complete tasks on time	( ) ( ) ( ) ( ) ( ) ( )	Cannot be counted on to have tasks completed on time
7. Can be counted on to complete tasks at a high quality level	( ) ( ) ( ) ( ) ( ) ( )	Cannot be counted on to complete tasks at a high quality level
8. Willing to work through conflict and negotiate solution	( ) ( ) ( ) ( ) ( ) ( )	Seeks to avoid conflict and confrontation
9. Can be relied on to follow team norms	( ) ( ) ( ) ( ) ( ) ( )	Cannot be relied on to follow team norms
10. Contributed an equitable part of the project tasks	( ) ( ) ( ) ( ) ( ) ( )	Did not contribute an equitable part of the project tasks

Provide an explanation for any item above that you rated on the right hand side of the column

Provide any additional relevant information for this evaluation:

Assemble Final Project Notebook

The final step in closing out your project is to assemble the final project notebook. Your team should have been compiling the project notebook throughout the project. However, this is your final opportunity to make sure that all documentation about how your team carried out the project is included in the notebook.

As stated in Chapter 3, the project notebook provides a history of how your team carried out its project. The notebook is important because it is the repository of all the team's work. As the repository, it provides documentation for the instructor and your team in assessing and evaluating how well the project was organized, planned, and managed.

In addition to submitting the notebook to the course instructor, it is advisable that each team member receives a copy of the notebook. This can later be used in the team member's portfolio and used to substantiate experience in teamwork when seeking employment opportunities.

Exercise 9.3. Compile Final Project Notebook

Compile the final project notebook. Usually the notebook contains the following documents:
- Team charter
- Project definition document
- Project Gantt chart
- Project resources and costs
- Communication plan
- Interim reports, filed chronologically
- Meeting agendas and minutes, filed chronologically

- Description of final product
- Team evaluation
- Individual evaluations (optional, depending on course instructions)
- Final product (optional, depending on course instructions).

The project notebook is submitted to the course instructor. Additional copies of the file may be provided to each team member. Alternatively, the notebook may be an electronic file.

Summary

A number of important activities are completed to close out a project. The evaluation documents and various reports provide a valuable history of the project that can be used to assess where things went right, where things went wrong, and where improvements should be made in future projects. The closeout is composed of the following action items:

- Holding final client meeting
- Preparing final project report
- Conducting post-project evaluation
- Performing individual team member evaluations
- Compiling the final project file

Chapter 10
Afterwards

Project closeouts usually end with a celebration recognizing the contribution and hard work that made the project a success. The team (or all the course teams) should plan a celebration together, perhaps pizza ordered in on the last day of class, dinner out, or meeting at a favorite gathering place on or near campus.

Part of what you are celebrating is being able to use the product your team created as part of your individual portfolio of samples of your work. This portfolio is invaluable when you are job seeking. Prospective employers like to see what they are getting before they hire. A portfolio that contains evidence of well-executed teamwork will put you on top of the competition. As a college professor, I encourage my students to keep such a portfolio. Those students that do this and present it to prospective employers usually get the job offer they want.

You are also celebrating the fact that you have learned a new skill set, one that is useful in every aspect of today's world. You can apply your team skills to other classroom teams, teaching other students how to manage their own classroom teams.

However, team skills are not limited to classroom or work-related teams. For example, you can use the conflict management techniques in everyday associations with family, friends, and professional interactions. Think about how you can reduce unhealthy conflict just by using the techniques you learned through your team process.

Your skills in managing a meeting are extremely practical to use for any type of meeting. For example, as a volunteer in a community group or church organization, you will probably be attending meetings or asked to chair meetings. Your skills will help your volunteer groups manage meetings more efficiently and productively. By now you should be an expert in meetings management, so why not conduct a workshop on managing meetings to help your volunteer group conduct effective meetings?

You can also use your problem-solving approach to manage a project. These skills aren't confined to work-related projects. Think about how useful your skills are for planning a project at home or for a volunteer organization.

Clearly, your team skills are valuable and will last a lifetime and this in itself is cause to celebrate your team experience.

Appendix A

Following are the answers to the group problem-solving test, "Lost on the Moon"

Items	NASA's Reasoning	NASA's Ranks	Your Ranks	Error Points	Group Ranks	Error Points
Box of matches	No oxygen to sustain flame, virtually worthless	15				
Food concentrate	Efficient means of supplying energy requirements	4				
Fifty feet of nylon rope	Useful in scaling cliffs, tying injured together	6				
Parachute silk	Protection from sun's rays	8				
Solar-powered portable heating unit	Not needed unless on dark side	13				
Two .45 caliber pistols	Possible means of self-propulsion	11				
One case of Pet milk	Bulkier duplication of food concentrate	12				
Two 100-pound tanks of oxygen	Most pressing survival need	1				
Stellar map (of the moon's constellations)	Primary means of navigation	3				
Self-inflating life raft	CO_2 bottle in military raft may be used for propulsion	9				
Magnetic compass	Magnetic field on moon is not polarized; worthless for navigation	14				
5 gallons of water	Replacement for tremendous liquid loss on lighted side	2				
Signal flares	Distress signal when mother ship is sighted	10				

Appendix B

Project Notebook

To organize, plan, and manage your project, you need to compile a project notebook. The purpose of the notebook is to catalog and maintain all documentation related to the project and to describe *how* the team accomplished the project. The notebook can be in paper form, such as a three-ring binder, or in electronic form.

Project Notebook Contents	
Binder Tab or Electronic Folder	**Contents**
Team Information	• Team member names and contact information • Team-Building Exercise • Team member personal styles
Team Charter	• Team Charter
Project Planning & Management	• Project-Definition Document • Gantt Chart • Task-Assignment Grid • Task-Resource Requirements • Communication Plan
Project Reports	• Interim Project Reports filed in chronological order
Project Meetings	• Meeting Agendas in chronological order • Meeting Minutes in chronological order
Evaluations	• Team evaluation • Individual evaluations (optional, depending on instructor directions)

Appendix C

Team Meeting Evaluation Form

Use the following form to evaluate each team meeting. For items where you respond "No," evaluate the underlying causes and take appropriate corrective action.

Meeting Date: Team members present:		
Meeting Process Item	**Yes**	**No**
Was there an agenda for the meeting?		
Was the agenda published according to meeting norms?		
Did the meeting start on time?		
Did the meeting end on time?		
Did all members arrive on time?		
Were minutes of the last meeting prepared and presented?		
Were all meeting norms as stated in the team charter followed?		
Was there a secretary to take minutes?		
Was there a timekeeper for the meeting?		
Was all meeting discussion relevant?		
Was the agenda followed?		
Were time frames on the agenda adequate?		
Did all members come prepared to the meeting?		
Did everyone present participate in the meeting discussions and decisions?		
Did the team make appropriate decisions?		
Was conflict handled effectively?		

Appendix D

Team Interim Assessments

Review your interim project reports and use the following checklist to evaluate how your team is managing the project. If your assessment turns up problems, it is important that your team correct them by identifying the underlying causes.

Assessment Date:		
Item	Yes	List Corrective Action if "No"
Is your team staying on schedule?		
Is each team member completing tasks on time?		
Are tasks for each team member equally distributed?		
Are tasks being completed at a quality level?		
Are appropriate resources available?		
Is the project staying within budget?		

Appendix E

Quick Reference Guide

Use the following guide as a quick reference for organizing and managing your student team.

Organize the Team	Solidify Team Belief using a team building exercise. Discuss the importance of team belief Determine personal styles of team members using a style inventory Assess your team's style diversity Develop a project notebook
Develop Team Charter	Name your team Establish team mission Identify team goals Establish team norms Assign team roles
Establish policies for conducting productive meetings	Set regular meeting times Establish meeting rules and control processes Establish role of team leader Establish role of team members Appoint secretary Appoint timekeeper Evaluate meeting control processes Develop and use conflict management techniques
Define the project	Develop project definition document that includes project: problem statement, name, description, scope, constraints, objectives, timeline, costs, resources, oversight.
Plan the project	Develop task list Develop task time frames Assign task responsibility Identify project resources and costs Develop communication plan
Manage the project	Conduct team meetings Evaluate project status Prepare interim reports
Project Closeout	Hold final client meeting Prepare final project report Conduct post-project evaluation Perform individual team member evaluations Assemble final project notebook

Appendix F

Technology Tools

You can use several technology tools to manage your student team. These tools can enhance your team's effectiveness.

Groupware. Groupware includes features such as online calendars, task managers, bulletin boards, group email, shared file space. Yahoo Groups, WebCT, and eCollege are some examples of groupware. You can use these technology tools in the several ways.

- Online calendar. Use for scheduling your team meetings, and task and deliverable due dates. A central calendar helps keep all team members organized.
- Task manager. Use for assigning tasks to team members and to track status and completion of tasks. A central task manager makes everyone aware of what work needs to be done and who is responsible for completing it. The task manager is a supplement to the Gantt chart, but does not replace it.
- Bulletin board. Use for posting messages or other information to all team members. This facilitates communication among all team members and ensures that everyone receives the same information.
- Group email. Sending one email that reaches all team members saves time. It also ensures that everyone gets the same information at the same time.
- Shared files. Posting electronic files in one place increases efficiency. All members have access to the same files to carry out their tasks. All members work off the same file, thus preventing problems arising having different versions of files.

Chat Rooms. Chat rooms provide the ability to have real time discussions electronically. Chat rooms can be used as an alternative when face-to-face meetings are not possible. Meeting norms developed by your team apply to chat room meetings, just as they do for face-to-face meetings. For example, the team leader facilitates the chat room meeting; members are expected to be on time to meetings; members are expected to participate in meetings; minutes are kept of meetings, and so on.

Conferencing Technology. Group conference calls are an alternative to face-to-face meetings. Remember that all meeting and conflict management norms apply to conference calls just as they apply to face-to-face meetings.

Index

CPSIA information can be obtained
at www.ICGtesting.com
Printed in the USA
LVOW07s2303070118
562194LV00001B/105/P

9 781430 313649